# Landscapes of Specific Literacies in Contemporary Society

This volume makes a timely contribution to our understanding of literacy as a multi-faceted, complexly situated activity. Each chapter provides the reader with a fresh perspective into a different site for literate behaviour, approaches, design and relationships and offers an exploration into the use of literacy theories to inform policy and practice, particularly in regard to curriculum.

Bringing together international experts in the field, the contributing authors represent a wide variety of theoretical and research perspectives which cover literacy in various forms, including:

- transformative literacy
- survey literacy
- academic literacies
- information literacy in the workplace
- digital literacy.

*Landscapes of Specific Literacies in Contemporary Society* suggests that literacy curriculum needs to evolve from its current perspective if it is to cater for the demands of the 21st-century contemporary globalised society. The book will be of key interest to researchers and academics in the fields of education, curriculum studies and the sociology of education, as well as to policy makers and literacy specialists.

**Vicky Duckworth** is Senior Lecturer and MA Co-ordinator in Post Compulsory Education and Training (PCET) and Schools' University Lead at Edge Hill University, UK.

**Gordon Ade-Ojo** is Principal Lecturer, Lifelong Learning Sector Network Coordinator and co-leader of the MA education programme at the University of Greenwich, UK.

# Routledge Research in Education

# Landscapes of Specific Literacies in Contemporary Society

## Exploring a social model of literacy

Edited by Vicky Duckworth and
Gordon Ade-Ojo

LONDON AND NEW YORK

First published 2015
by Routledge
2 Park Square, Milton Park, Abingdon, Oxon OX14 4RN

and by Routledge
711 Third Avenue, New York, NY 10017

*Routledge is an imprint of the Taylor & Francis Group, an informa business*

*British Library Cataloguing in Publication Data*
A catalogue record for this book is available from the British Library

*Library of Congress Cataloging in Publication Data*
A catalog record for this book has been requested

ISBN: 978-0-415-74124-8 (hbk)
ISBN: 978-1-315-81538-1 (ebk)

Typeset in Bembo
by Swales and Willis Ltd., Exeter, Devon, UK

Printed and bound in Great Britain by
TJ International Ltd, Padstow, Cornwall

This book is dedicated to Professor Mary Hamilton whose wisdom, compassion, creativity, bravery and drive have flourished and led the way in the field of practitioner research, literacies and social justice.

# Contents

# Figures

# Contributors

**Gordon Ade-Ojo** is a principal lecturer in the School of Education at the University of Greenwich. His research has been connected with the exploration of adult literacy policy and how this has impacted on practice. His research interests focus on the perception of literacy as social practice. Gordon has published several articles, book chapters and books and currently contributes to teaching and supervision on the PGCE, MA and doctoral programmes at the University of Greenwich. Gordon is a research associate of the University of South Africa (UNISA) and a co-editor of *IJMCS*.

**David Barton** is Professor of Language and Literacy in the Department of Linguistics at Lancaster University. His research has mainly been concerned with carrying out detailed studies of everyday literacies; exploring the relations of literacy and learning; and rethinking the nature of literacy, especially in the online world. His most recent books are *Language online* (with Carmen Lee, 2013) and *Researching language and social media* (co-authored, 2014), both published by Routledge.

**Lynn Coleman** is a senior lecturer at Cape Peninsula University of Technology in South Africa where she also has an academic staff development role. She recently completed her PhD at the Open University in the United Kingdom. Her research interests include academic literacies within the vocational higher education context; literacies associated with visual communication and media courses; and curriculum design and development. Her research and publications highlight the complexity of literacies in the curriculum context and suggest how knowledge within different domains are articulated and brought into being across vocational curricula in higher education.

**John Crawford** was the founder and director of the Scottish Information Literacy Project and now leads its successor project, an online community of practice, Information Skills for a 21st Century Scotland (http://scotinfo lit.squarespace.com). He has authored over 85 articles in professional and academic journals on information literacy, the evaluation of library and information services and library and information history, has written three books and contributed chapters to others. He has guest edited two special issues of the American academic journal, *Library Trends* and guest edited a special issue of *Library and Information Research* on the theme of information literacy and lifelong learning.

**Vicky Duckworth** is a senior lecturer and senior research fellow at Edge Hill University where she also holds the role of Schools' University Partnership. Throughout her career, Vicky has published several works on a range of issues and research topics. These topics include: critical and emancipatory approaches to education; widening participation; Further Education teaching and learning; social justice, literacies and community engagement. Her recent research has been published in her book *Learning trajectories, violence and empowerment among adult basic skills learners* (Routledge, 2013).

**Mary Hamilton** is Professor of Adult Learning and Literacy in the Department of Educational Research at Lancaster University. She is a founding member of the Research and Practice in Adult Literacy group. She researches and writes in the areas of literacy policy and governance, practitioner enquiry, everyday literacy practices and change.

**Mark Hepworth** is a reader in People's Information Behaviour at the Centre for Information Management at Loughborough University. Mark is particularly interested in how we can help to develop people's capacity to exploit knowledge, data and information as individuals and also within an organisational or community context. His research, PhD supervision and teaching reflects this interest and includes: developing theoretical frameworks and applied methodologies in information literacy; e-literacy; information needs analysis; people's information seeking and use behaviour; learning and pedagogy; people centred design; participative design; community engagement and effective ways to plan, monitor and evaluate i-capacity interventions.

**Mary R. Lea** is reader in Academic and Digital Literacies at the Open University, UK. Her wide-ranging research is concerned with social and cultural approaches to the writing and reading practices of both students and academics. Recently, she has turned this lens towards the relationship between literacies and technologies in higher education and challenged some of the more dominant discourses commonly associated with digital literacy. Her publications include (with Robin Goodfellow), *Challenging elearning in the university: a literacies perspective* (SRHE/McGraw Hill 2007) and *Literacy in the digital university: critical perspectives on learning, scholarship and technology* (SRHE/Routledge 2013).

**Guy Merchant** is Professor of Literacy in Education at Sheffield Hallam University, UK, where he specialises in research into digital literacy in formal and informal educational settings. He has published widely in international journals and is a founding editor of the *Journal of Early Childhood Literacy*. With Julia Davies he co-authored the influential book *Web 2.0 for schools: learning and social participation* (Peter Lang, 2009). He is lead editor of *Virtual literacies* (Routledge, 2013) and a contributing editor for *New literacies around the globe* (Routledge, 2014).

# Chapter 1

# Introduction

## Is practice keeping pace with policy?

*Gordon Ade-Ojo and Vicky Duckworth*

Literacy over the ages has been an embodiment of a trinity: perceptions/theory, policy and practice. Each part of the trinity has somehow informed the emergence of the other parts of the trinity. However, the relationship between the three components of this trinity has not necessarily been consistent. In some cases, theories and perceptions have been shown to be greatly influential in the shaping of practice. In other cases, however, the dominant relationship has been that between policy and practice. Nonetheless, that varied pattern of relationships amongst these components of a trinity has endured over generations of literacy development and evolution. Association amongst the elements of the trinity appears to have varied from period to period as demonstrated below.

In the early medieval period, the dominant perception was of literacy as 'primary orality' (Houston, 2002:1). That perception informed the conception of literacy practice and policy which considered writing and reading – a limited perception of literacy as it were – as 'skills possessed by a few professionals, while the bulk of the population relied for information on what they could see and what they could hear' (Houston, 2002:1). Such a perception's influence on both policy and practice was highly significant. Policies were designed to provide solely for the select few while practice focused on the specific needs of the select few. As a result, literacy at this time became a restricted species with an aura of inaccessibility attached to literacy practices such as writing.

By the early modern period, however, the perception of literacy had evolved and contributed to a different policy direction as well as practice. A different set of interests bore upon literacy during this period and, as such, its shape and delivery began to alter (Stone, 1969, Craig, 1981 and Houston, 2002). Encapsulating these changing interests which influenced the perceptions of literacy during the early modern period, Stone notes 'The structure of education in a society is determined by . . . Social stratification, job opportunities, religion, theories of social control, demographic and social patterns, economic organisation and resources, and finally political theory and institutions' (Stone 1969:70, Houston, 2002:2). The complexities inherent in these influences meant that both policy and practice in respect of literacy began to develop into more complex structures. As noted by McLuhan (1973), a need for different types of new literacies has developed as the influences and perceptions change with a movement towards what Houston refers to as 'secondary orality' (p.2).

In more recent times, the relationship amongst the components of the trinity has become even more obvious. In the recent past in the UK, literacy development can be classified into three eras: 70s to mid-80s; mid-80s to late 90s and late 90s to the present (Ade-Ojo, 2008). In these eras, various patterns of relationship amongst the components of the trinity were also evident. While some scholars have described the 1970s as lacking a definitive literacy policy (see e.g. Limage 1987:293), others differ from this view. For instance, Hamilton and Hillier (2006) suggest that adult literacy was first identified as a national policy issue in the UK in the mid-1970s. This conflict in perceptions can be resolved if policy initiatives in the 70s are recognised as originating from, and driven mostly by, non-governmental stakeholders. The 1970s can, therefore, be seen as an era of practice-driven policy, in which a myriad of initiatives mostly originated from practitioners and their funders. Informing several of these contributions were various socio-cognitive themes which emanated from an aggregation of the contributors' social reality.

In the 1970s there was very little evidence that there was any serious policy awareness of the principles embodied in any major theoretical framework of literacy. This is not surprising as the currently dominant theoretical concepts such as the social model of literacy and New Literacies can be considered 'latter day' developments. The notion of literacy as a social practice was something that at this point was not consciously engaged with by either practitioners or policy makers. However, in the context of the perception of the era as one in which policy was led by practice, the relationship amongst the three elements of the trinity is embodied in the role of one of the leading practitioner organisations, the Adult Literacy Resource Agency (ALRA). ALRA, in fact, appeared to have subscribed, consciously or unconsciously, to some elements of the principles of New Literacies, particularly the argument that there are many literacies and that literacy is a social practice. One of the pre-occupations of ALRA was the development of work-specific literacies. In ALRA (1976:4), this accidental or conscious alignment to the ethos of New Literacies was emphasised with the declaration that: 'Literacy is an essential tool of vocational education and training and allocations of money for training could, we believe, validly be used to extend the provision for adult literacy in vocational context'. While this echoes in part the traditional perception of literacy, it also recognises one of the main tenets of New Literacies, which perceives literacy as a social practice situated in different social spheres (Barton, Hamilton and Ivanič 2000). In this respect, the world of work is seen as the main social sphere for which literacy needed to be developed and utilised. Nevertheless, there is some evidence that policy and practice at the time was shaped by elements of what is now generally referred to as New Literacies.

Similarly, there is evidence that some providers and practitioners aligned to the principles of critical literacy. In particular, Freire's emancipatory model of literacy (1970) appears to have been the driving force behind the practice of many centres and practitioners. In many cases, these providers and practitioners manoeuvred in spite of increasingly difficult conditions and used a combination of creativity and adaptation to continue to promote their preferred model of literacy (Duckworth, 2013). Typifying providers in this class are: Brighton Friends' Centre who used the publication of *Write First Time* to empower their learners (Tuckett, 2001) and Gatehouse which utilised a similar principle. What was most important about these organisations at the time was that they provided the opportunity for many practitioners to keep their perspectives. For this era, therefore, while there were no explicit declarations in terms of theoretical allegiances, there was evidence that both policy and practice were intertwined with elements of some theoretical perceptions of literacy thus upholding the trinity argument.

In the 1980s to mid-90s era, the practice and policy of literacy moved from what might be described as a critical/social model back into what can be described as the traditional/cognitive model of literacy. With the ascendancy of the skills and employability agendas, literacy policy and practice affiliated with the traditional model of literacy. This alignment is informed by two reasons. In this respect, the justification argument as presented by Hildyard and Olson (1978) takes a central role. One of the central issues in their justification of the traditional/cognitive model of literacy is the fact that 'it legitimises the extraordinary efforts and resources that go into compulsory schooling' (p.4). While this might address compulsory schooling specifically, the concept of justification was extended to literacy as a whole. As argued by Street (1984:19) 'The qualities which they attribute to literacy thus take on a more general significance of justifying the vast expense on Western education systems'. With the gradual increase in the funds made available for literacy over this period, it became inevitable that the gate-keepers of the funds, the various quangos and organisations like MSC, TECS, FEFC and ALBSU, would subscribe to a model of literacy that justified their outlay. Thus, through the intervention of funders and other regulatory quangos who prescribed the literacy curriculum and the modality of its delivery, the traditional/cognitive literacy model gained ascendancy in the 1980s and 1990s. The instrument for dispensing this model was closely linked to the assessment regimes that were introduced. Many of the assessments available were competence-based and therefore had specific outcomes attached to them. This structure is itself complementary to the structure of the traditional/cognitive model of literacy which considers literacy to be a set of cognitive skills. This synergy then formed another basis for the dominance of the traditional/cognitive model of literacy. For this era, therefore, there was a more explicitly patterned relationship between perceptions of literacy, literacy policy and practice. What is even more significant is the fact that all three components of the trinity appeared to have kept pace with one another although, in many cases, the imposition of the traditional model of literacy created tension between practitioners and funders. As noted by Fowler

(2005:125), 'there was a sense of political dissent between the practitioners who were involved in community publishing, with their associated notions of learner empowerment, and the government funded agency'. Unfortunately for the practitioners, the agencies were considerably more powerful as they held the purse strings and eventually saw off other models of literacy that were proposed by practitioners. The period between the 1980s and mid-1990s therefore saw a more pronounced synergy amongst the trinity with the entrenchment of the government-favoured traditional/cognitive model of literacy.

By the 1990s there was a reduction in LEA funding and control. Instead, basic skills were given statutory status through a more formal further education (FE) system which was dependent on funding through a national funding body, the Further Education Funding Council (FEFC) (see Hamilton and Hillier 2006). At the heart of the more recent era in the evolution of literacy policy and practice, between the late 90s and the present, is the Moser Committee. Drawing from the policy generated by the work of the committee, it is very evident that practice has in this case been significantly shaped by policy. In a report on the workings of the Moser Committee, Ade-Ojo (2011) established that there was a range of factors that affected many of the decisions taken in the committee, effectively resulting in the adult literacy policy being embedded in the Skills for Life agenda. While some of these factors impacted directly on members of the committee and their agenda, others impacted in a rather indirect way. What the findings of the study did was to confirm the hypothesis that the factors that informed policy development at the time of the Moser committee had evolved in the same manner that the policy itself had evolved. As such, it has helped to confirm the argument that policy evolution went in tandem with the evolution of influential factors. In other words, adult literacy policy has evolved from the influence of factors related to the needs of learners in the 1970s to the influence of factors more recognised from the viewpoint of the funders: the government.

Evidence suggests that the most important factors in the evolution of adult literacy policy were the economy, employment and international competitiveness. These themes were continuously found to have been influential on the committee's deliberations, either through a pre-determined government agenda, or through the socio-cognitive realities that members of the committee brought to the policy-making process. The influence of these factors on policy making undoubtedly had significant influence on practice.

The legacy of the Moser Committee-led era was the total dominance of policy over practice. By implication, this suggests the silencing of theory and perceptions of literacy. This is a paradox given that this is the era in which many scholarly engagements with literacy perceptions began to dominate. Since Street's seminal contributions (1984, 1993) on the autonomous and ideological models of literacy, voices on perceptions and models of literacy have persistently echoed across the world. Contributions from Barton (1994) on the ecology of language, Barton, Hamilton and Ivanič (2000) on social literacy, Gee (1998a and 1998b), Lankshear (1999), Luke (1992) and indeed the New Literacies group, have been consistent with the  message that perceptions of literacy must take into account the social nature of literacy which must, therefore, be seen as a social practice. Such a perception must also be reflected in practice in terms of the curriculum and the learning outcomes associated with it. Demonstration of the achievement of these learning outcomes is situated in the learners' real lives and everyday practices. Teaching and learning resources can be developed by the learner to capture and give meaning to their experience, motivation and aspirations, or co-produced with the teacher (see McNamara, 2007; Duckworth, 2008; Duckworth, 2009) rather than arising from a prescriptive pre-set curriculum. Learners' histories and biographies can impact on their learning environments (Duckworth, 2013). The curriculum moves towards a *caring, critical, co-construction model* (CCCM) based on a social approach. As such, teachers' awareness and sensitivity to the issues that learners bring into the classroom and the development of strategies for dealing with them effectively is important if the barriers are to be addressed (Barton, Hamilton and Ivanič, 2000: 137). This may entail therapeutic interventions for those who are most vulnerable such as those with mental-health issues and/or physical disabilities. Indeed, literacy education has been shown to enhance confidence, contribute to personal development, promote health, social and political participation and lead to benefits in the public and private domains of learners' lives (Duckworth, 2013).

In spite of this abundance of contributions on the theoretical front, theory appears to have failed to keep pace with practice. There is little doubt that the dominant component of the trinity at this stage has remained policy. Practice has continued to be governed by policy which is perhaps even more entrenched because of the funding associated to it and perhaps because of the different perceptions of literacy held by policy makers. The crucial questions, therefore, must be: What is the impact of the social perception of literacy theories on the practice of adult literacy? In what ways have these perceptions shaped practice? While there is evidence that scholars of this inclination have offered some pedagogical suggestions, these have remained just that, suggestions. Could the social models have had more impact on practice? This volume is one of the steps towards answering that question in the affirmative. Contributions to this volume map out how a perception of literacy as a social practice can allow us to map out different curriculum and impact areas of focus in the practice of adult literacy. Each contribution focuses on a particular area and offers a description of how the concept of multi-literacies is manifested in the ways in which literacies can be specific for each of these areas. The underpinning argument that drives this book, therefore, is a call for the recognition of literacy curricula for specific purposes which in effect make the argument around social literacy more functional. It takes the social model of literacy from the level of mere theoretical postulations to a level of exploring its relevance in practice with a particular focus on the curriculum. In tandem with the recognition of the fact that literacy should be seen as reflecting distinct social practices, this book argues for distinct literacy curricula for distinct social practices.

The suggestion of distinct literacy curricula immediately evokes the age-long philosophical debate and dichotomy between the Aristotelian concept of curriculum which pits Plato's art of the dialectician that involves 'holding together both the one and the many' against the Aristotelian view which emphasises the necessity of 'eliminating contradictions by choosing whether a person has a characteristic or not' (Whitehead, 1999). The philosophical essence of the contemporary literacy curriculum renders it a complication along the Platonic construct and, therefore, enables it to dominate other potential constructs. The focus of this book is to show that proponents of the social model of literacy must, like Aristotle, embrace a non-contradictory construct by developing specific curricula for specific practices such that they are able to foreground the social characteristics of literacy.

The engagement with distinction of literacy curricula consequently evokes Hirst's dated but highly relevant engagement with disciplinary knowledge. Hirst's discipline thesis in curriculum theory argues that knowledge must come in 'form' which is 'a distinct way in which our experience becomes structured round the use of accepted public symbols' (1974: 38). Developing from this, the notion of literacy for specific purposes (which this book is designed to advocate) argues for a disciplinary development of literacy curricula such that each discipline, together with the vocation and profession aligned to it, is seen as a social practice.

Without such a disciplinary distinction, literacy practice has been dominated by the curriculum of a single social practice and this has effectively led to the much decried dominance. So, although there have been many outcries by the proponents of the sociological approach to literacy, it has remained more of 'literacy in theory and less of literacy in practice'. The result is the dominance of the cognitive model leading to what Gee, Hull and Lankshear (1996: xiii) famously referred to as 'creating new social identities or new kinds of people'. What this book hopes to achieve is to draw on the principle of creating new identities to create 'new literate people'. The underpinning argument being that if literacy curricula are shaped around specific disciplines and, therefore, specific social practices that many within society are socially aligned to, opportunities for creating a new socially literate society will emerge. Therefore, this book aims to map out a theoretical framework for utilising the principles of a sociocultural approach to literacy in curriculum development by focusing on disciplinary characteristics. The salient question in this respect is; how can we make literacy social in practice? The contributions in this book have provided some insight into how this is being done in various contexts.

In Chapter 1, Ade-Ojo and Duckworth track the relationship between literacy theory, practice and policy. Using this as a background for this volume, they argue that the three elements have interchangeably informed each other although this influence varies from period to period. Having explored such a relationship in various generations, they suggest that in the contemporary setting, the elements of this trinity have not kept pace with each other. On the basis of this, they set the scene for the exploration of LSP, which they argue, underpins much of the contributions to this volume, and which illustrates how practice is now beginning to attempt to catch up with theory.

In Chapter 2, Ade-Ojo presents a theoretical rationale for the reconstruction of literacy curriculum in order for it to respond to the challenges of the twenty-first century. He draws on existing literature and evidence from practice to argue that the so-called dominance of a cognitive model is promoted by the lack of a functional social model which is open to accountability. Based on this, the chapter argues for a specific literacy curriculum model as a way of functionally representing the social model of literacy in curriculum development. It anchors this claim to linguistic, anthropological and educational theories. Finally, the construct of specific literacies is anchored to the overall framework of the social model of literacy, highlighting how the features of the latter are manifested in the former.

In Chapter 3, Vicky Duckworth argues that New Literacy Studies and critical approaches to education offer a potential space for transformation whereby basic-skills learners can explore their narratives and society around them. This shifts from a traditional, competency based approach to curriculum design to a culturally relevant, learner-driven and socially empowering model which takes into consideration the cultural, psychological and educational factors related to the learners and their lives. Drawing on research from educational and community-based settings, this chapter argues that the aforementioned encourages dialogic communication between teachers and literacy learners whereby learners and communities can ask questions, analyse and subsequently work through effective and meaningful strategies to take agency over their lives, enhancing their situation and empowering them and the local and wider communities.

In Chapter 4, Mary Hamilton argues that international surveys of literacy have become increasingly important over the last 20 years. The surveys are organized by a range of agencies including the Organization for Economic Co-operation and Development (OECD), UNESCO and the European Union. National governments commit considerable funding to the surveys which induce participants to compare themselves against one another other using the results. Mary argues that curricula, performance indicators and assessments are shaped by these measures and that in this process, our views of what counts as literacy, its goals and of literacy learners are also formed. Standardised profiles of achievement are highly valued while at the same time perceived to be at odds with the everyday literacy practices of both teachers and their students. This chapter describes some of the background to these tests, how they are constructed and the rationales used for them. It argues that a critical engagement with them is essential for anyone currently working in literacy education. In the peculiarity of literacy employed for these surveys, Mary highlights another dimension to literacy as the social practice.

In Chapter 5, Lynn Coleman and Mary R. Lea examine what research into academic literacies can contribute to a changing higher education. The field of academic literacies emerged at a particular historical moment in the 1990s against the backdrop of widening access to higher education for groups of students who had previously been marginalized from participating in the university. Its main focus was on student writing and making visible the gaps between students' and university teachers' understanding of meaning-making in written assignments. Over the last twenty years the field has moved beyond its initial concern with undergraduate writing practices to embrace a diverse range of new contexts in and around the academy as academic, disciplinary and professional boundaries shift and blur and, in addition, as new technologies enable new forms of textual knowledge making practices both within and outside the academy. They argue that we are only beginning to understand the complexity of the emergence of these new textual practices and the implications in terms of meaning making and the curriculum. Using examples from the UK and South Africa this chapter revisits the foundational principles of academic literacies research and examines their relevance for understanding teacher and student practices around text production in the context of today's twenty-first-century higher education.

In Chapter 6, Mark Hepworth engages with the question 'How does the concept "workplace information literacy" enable us to reflect on information literacy and can it be viewed from an individual, organisational or social perspective?' His chapter provides a brief overview of some of the key themes evident in the information literacy literature and demonstrates that the concept is still evolving and is now beginning to reflect ontological distinctions made in other disciplines. Initially the primary focus was the individual and their information skills and had a behavioural orientation. At this point the concept was generally associated with the use of information sources in libraries. Gradually we have seen the concept evolve and take on different meanings partly because it has been discussed within other contexts such as everyday life, the community and the workplace. The social dimension of information literacy has become a more common theme. Drawing on research from educational, community-based and organisational settings this chapter discusses these themes and argues that these are levels of abstraction, or lenses that help to appreciate the complexities of information literacy, both within and outside the workplace.

In Chapter 7, John Crawford focusses on repurposing information literacy for the twenty-first century. As a start, he explores the term 'information literacy' which for him means the use, evaluation and repurposing of information for a wide range of purposes. The chapter provides an overview and synthesises these developments in a lifelong learning context and suggests that the definition of information literacy must be modified to take account of key policy documents like the Prague Declaration (2003) and the Alexandria Proclamation (2005) which identify information literacy as a civil and skills right. The increasingly dominant influence of the information society is also considered. The implications for information literacy policy and curriculum development and the options available for action within states are discussed.

In Chapter 8, Guy Merchant invites us to move with the times. He traces the emergence of mobile and digital devices and beyond from the early days of networked technology, to an era when computers were things one had to locate, as they were in particular places such as labs and suites and then later in offices, classrooms and homes. He argues that although this location-specific computing is still very common, the rapid take-up of mobile devices invites new practices; it changes our relationships with one another and makes novel ways of meaning-making possible. Thinking about the implications of this latest shift for the literacies of educational institutions, learners and teachers has only just begun. This chapter ultimately explores how educators might respond to the widespread take-up of powerful handheld technologies. It takes a look back to the social dimension of literacy in the context of childhood learners.

In Chapter 9, David Barton offers a theoretical analysis of the previous chapters in response to the changing landscape of literacy. He draws conclusions on the ways in which we must respond to the demands of the twenty-first century, how we must position literacy through specific curricula in order to make it acceptable to funders and to enable it to meet the impending and emergent challenges. Drawing on the chapters his key theme is 'what's next?'.

## References

Ade-Ojo, G. O. (2008) Significant factors and events in the evolution of adult literacy policy and practice in the UK from the 70s to Moser. PhD thesis, University of Greenwich.

Ade-Ojo, G. O. (2011) 'Practitioners' perception of the impact of the vision of policy-makers on practice: the example of the recommendations of the Moser Commission', *Research Papers in Education*, 26(1): 53–77.

Adult Literacy Resource Agency (ALRA) (1976) Volume 8. London: HMSO.

Barton, D. (1994) *An introduction to the ecology of written language*. Oxford: Blackwell Publishing.

Barton, D., Hamilton, M. & Ivanic, R. (eds.) (2000) *Situated literacies: reading and writing in context*. London and New York: Routledge.

Craig, J. (1981) 'The expansion of education', *Review of Research in Education*, 9: 151–213.

Duckworth, K. (2008) *The influence of context on attainment in primary school: interactions between children, family and school contexts* (Wider Benefits of Learning Research Report no.28), London: Institute of Education, Centre for Research on the Wider Benefits of Learning.

Duckworth, V. (2009) *On the job: car mechanic tutor resources*, On the job 14–19 series. Warrington: Gatehouse Books.

Duckworth, V. (2010) 'Sustaining learning over time: it looks more like a Yellow Brick Road than a straightforward path for women experiencing violence', *Research and Practice in Adult Literacy*, 71: 19–20.

Duckworth, V. (2013) *Learning Trajectories, violence and empowerment amongst adult basic skills learners*. London: Routledge.

Duckworth, V. and Taylor, K. (2008) 'Words are for everyone', *Research and Practice in Adult Literacy*, 64: 30–328.

Fowler, Z. (2005) 'History of Adult Literacy campaigns' in Fowler, Z. Politically constructing adult literacy: A case study of the Skills for Life strategy for improving adult literacy in England 1997–2002. PhD thesis, Institute of Education, London.

Freire, P. (1970) *Pedagogy of the Oppressed*. London: Penguin Books.

Gee, J. P. (1998a) 'The new literacy studies and the "social turn"'. Madison: University of Winsconsin-Madison Department of curriculum and instruction. (Mimeo)

Gee, J. P. (1998b) 'Preamble to literacy program'. Madison: University of Winsconsin-Madison Department of curriculum and instruction. (Mimeo)

Gee, J., Hull, G. & Lankshear, C. (1996) *The new work order: behind the language of the new capitalism*. Boulder, CO: Westview Press.

Hamilton, M. & Hillier, Y. (2006*) Changing faces of adult literacy, language and numeracy: a critical history*. Stoke-on-Trent and Sterling, UK: Trentham Books.

Hildyard, A. & Olson, D. (1978) 'Literacy and the specialisation of language' Unpublished manuscript, Ontario Institute for Studies in Education. (Referred to in Street, 1984).

Hirst, P. (1974) *Knowledge and the curriculum*. London: Routledge & Kegan Paul.

Houston, R. (2002) *Literacy in early modern Europe*. Harlow: Pearson Education.

Lankshear, C. (1999) 'Literacy in education: disciplined developments in a post-disciplinary age' in Peters, M. *After the Disciplines*. Westport, CT: Greenwood Press.

Limage, J. L. (1987) 'adult literacy policy in industrialised countries' in Arnove, R. F. & Graff, H. J. (eds.) *National Literacy Campaigns*. New York: Plenum Publishing Corporation.

Luke, A. (1992) 'Literacy and work in new times'. *Open Letter* 3(1): 3–15.

McLuhan, M. (1973) *Understanding media*. London: Abacus.

McNamara, M. (2007) *Getting better*. Warrington: Gatehouse Books.

Stone, L. (1969) 'Literacy and Education in England, 1640–1900', *Past and Present*, 42: 69–1139.

Street, B. (1984) *Literacy in theory and practice*. Cambridge: Cambridge University Press.

Street, B. (1993) *Cross-cultural approaches to literacy*. Cambridge: Cambridge University Press.

Tuckett, A. (2001) 'If I can't dance . . . convivality and adult learners'. Lecture presented at the University of East London as NIACE chairman, January 2001.

Whitehead, J. (1999) 'Educative relations in a new era', *Pedagogy, Culture and Society*, 7(1): 73–90.

# Chapter 2

# Towards a functional curriculum model of social literacy

## Literacy for specific purposes

*Gordon Ade-Ojo*

## Introduction

Perhaps the most consistent conclusions of contemporary academic engagement with the adult literacy discourse are first, that there are alternative perceptions of literacy, variously referred to as a social/ ideological model (Street, 1984 and 1993), and a sociological perception of literacy (Gee et al, 2006, Luke, 2005) and second, literacy policy and practice is dominated by a cognitive perception of literacy (Ade-Ojo, 2009 and 2011, Hamilton and Hillier, 2006, Lankshear and Gee, 1997, Street, 1993). This model, it is generally agreed, has failed many young and older people who have been classified as 'illiterate' because of their failure to acquire it. Almost equally consistent is the seemingly unending complaints of employers on the inadequacy of the literacy skills of young people (Ade-Ojo, 2009), and the government's lamentation on the lack of literacy and numeracy skills amongst young people who are pejoratively labelled as 'Not in Employment, Education or Training' (NEETs).

In spite of this seeming unanimity, very little has been offered towards reversing the dominance of the so-called cognitive model in policy making and practice. Most contributions on the relevance of alternative models have focussed on the instructional and pedagogical fronts (see e.g. Janks, 2000, Evans, 2005, Purcell-Gates, Degener, Jacobson and Soler, 2009) and on a reinforcement of the argument mapping out the theoretical bounds of these alternative models (see e.g. Street, 1983 and 1995, Gee 1996 and 2000). Indeed, no social model informed curriculum has been offered as an alternative to this dominant but often labelled ineffective model. In this paper, I shall set out to accomplish a number of things in relation to the continued dominance of the cognitive model and to advance the course of the social model of literacy. In other words, the goal of this paper is to promote rather than denounce the social model of literacy. Within this context, the ultimate vision is to advocate for its functionality through the advancement of a set of principles for its application to curriculum development.

Specifically, I shall endeavour to: offer explanations on why the dominant model has endured both in theory and practice for so long; propose a curriculum model which can both challenge the dominant traditional model of literacy curriculum and by implication, further the course of the social model; highlight the underpinning principles of the proposed model which essentially derive from the principles of social literacy; offer justifications for its existence; explore how this new model might benefit learners and chart out potential challenges that might emerge from adopting this new model of adult curriculum. Before engaging with these tasks, it is important to establish here that reference to literacy curriculum here is to literacy beyond school literacy and as such more relevant for adult literacy.

## Why is the dominant so dominant?

In a recent report, the OECD News Room (2013a) delivered a damning report, particularly on the literacy levels of young people noting that:

> [ . . . ] in England and the United States, the literacy and numeracy skills of young people entering the labour market are no better than those leaving for retirement. England ranks among the top three countries surveyed for literacy skills among the 55–65 year-olds. But the country is in the bottom three when it comes to such skills among 16–25 year-olds. American 55–65 year-olds perform around the average, but young Americans rank the lowest among their peers in the 24 countries surveyed.

This alarming report immediately raises a number of questions. First, why is it that two of the most socially and technologically advanced countries in the world present such a demeaning state of literacy competence amongst their young people? Second, what kind of tool has the OECD used in measuring the literacy levels of the countries they evaluated in their study? While the jury is still out on the answer to the former, the answer to the latter is relatively easy to access. The OECD's 2013 report makes it clear that the instrument for measuring literacy levels across countries is the specifically designed OECD programme for the international assessment of adult competencies (PIAAC).

The underpinning driver of PIAAC suggests that:

> Literacy is the ability to identify, understand, interpret, create, communicate and compute, using printed and written materials associated with varying contexts. Literacy involves a continuum of learning in enabling individuals to achieve their goals, to develop their knowledge and potential, and to participate fully in their community and wider society. (OECD, 2013b:1)

The emphasis on 'using printed and written materials', suggests that literacy must be embodied in a particular form. This, in my view, is the essence of the dominance of a particular perception of literacy. The imposition of such a view of what constitutes literacy is just one of many possible illustrations of why the dominant model of literacy – the autonomous model – has remained dominant for so long. How this dominance can be challenged through theoretical and practical engagement is my major concern in this chapter. Salient questions in this context are: What have the proponents of the alternative models done in order to upstage this dominance? What tools have we created to help relax the stranglehold that this model has on policy development and practice in the field of adult literacy?

Colins and Blot (2003:7) encapsulated the apprehension that drives the proposal in this chapter when they identified that the engagement with the dominance of the autonomous model, particularly by the New Literacy Studies group, is somewhat flawed in that although such understandings (as proposed by the proponents of the ideological/autonomous model of literacy) have a more general intellectual value . . . 'it is insufficient for re-thinking inherited values'. In essence, most of the contributions have been limited to the intellectual and theoretical realm and have, therefore, not really explored what can be done. It seems to me that the way to respond to this state of affairs is by establishing empowering instruments of the ideological model.

## Three explanations

There have been a range of explanations offered for the dominance of the autonomous model of literacy. I have, however, classified these into two broad categories which I have labelled the socio-psychological and the pedagogical explanations. Typifying the former is the argument of Gee (2001) who invokes the concept of 'dominant secondary discourses', which conflicts with and dominates the various other primary discourses. In this context, Gee notes, 'every act of speaking, writing, and behaving a linguist does as a linguist is meaningful only against the background of the whole social institution of linguistics and that institution is made up of concrete things like people, books and buildings'. This dominance, I argue, is of such potency that it is difficult to establish other discourses. Gee transfers this phenomenon to literacy and attempts to account for the dominance of one type of literacy over others with the notion of socio-psychological dominance. This construct highlights how certain literacies place us in certain roles in society. For him, it is the social function associated with the autonomous model that not only induces a psychological bond with it by the vast majority of learners, practitioners and policy makers, but also ensures its dominance. The prominence accorded this model through its use by the highly influential OECD (as discussed earlier) is an illustration of how the model has been placed on a prominent social pedestal.

In my view, however, this merely grapples with a question of perceptions and echoes what Colins and Blot (2003) classify as intellectualisation. How do we reverse this dominance? A reliance on an explanation that is built around socio-psychological factors simply stalls the debate. How do we move from the level of mere understanding as proposed by Gee to effecting a reversal? It is perhaps this typically pro-intellectual engagement that has led Brandt and Clinton (2002:1) to raise the spectre of what they call 'the limits of the local'. Merely understanding cannot break the hold that this model has on policy and practice. The productive way forward is to carve out a functional alternative to this functional dominance. This is what we as advocates of the social model have failed to do.

The latter form of explanation typified by Street (1995, 2005 and 2012) is more pragmatic and focuses more on how the dominance of the autonomous model is entrenched through education. This is perhaps more relevant here, as this chapter is particularly concerned with using the curriculum to respond to the dominance. While exploring the dominance of the autonomous model, Street (1995:24) notes that this state of dominance does 'force us to question whether the current framework in which such activities are conducted is the most fruitful'. Such a questioning stance forces us to review our understanding of the nature and the rationales for the dominance of the autonomous model which has been hugely decried and discredited. Street, therefore, argues that the dominance of the autonomous model is due mainly to two reasons: 1) the 'pedagogization' of literacy which has been achieved through the institutionalisation of the dominant model in the process of teaching and learning, and 2) the conflation of literacy practices with 'schooling or pedagogy' (1995:111).

While there is no questioning the credibility of Street's argument here, I argue that his description of the factors responsible for this dominance is not far-reaching enough. In place of what Street calls 'pedagogization', I offer the concept of 'curricularization'. This suggests that the major source of empowerment of the autonomous model is the fact that literacy curricula have been built around this model. Hence, as both Street and Gee have argued, the dominant model of literacy has been the fulcrum around which all accepted literacy curricula are built. This, in my view, is a more compelling and empirical explanation than, for example, Gee's socio-psychological account. I use the term curricularization here as a derivative of the word curriculum which has been defined variously as a product, a process and as praxis (Cornbleth, 2000). In this context, I use the term curriculum in a form that integrates the three perceptions of it referred to above. In essence, therefore, I see the process of curricularization as one which involves the pedagogical process, which is what I interpret Street's notion of pedagogization to mean; product, which embodies the content of learning; and praxis, which brings in the attitudinal dimension to programme development.

In respect of the conflation thesis offered by Street, the conclusion he reaches was to the effect that 'literacy need not be associated with schooling or pedagogy' (1995:112). In contrast, I argue that associating literacy with schooling is not the issue. Rather, it is the exclusion of other forms of literacy from schools that is crucial. In other words, the challenge for us should be how other forms of literacy can be conflated with schooling in order to temper the dominance of the autonomous model. What we must, however, do in addition to this, is buoy the chances of survival of other literacies by providing curricula to support their development, delivery and recognition. This will inevitably provide opportunities for accountability which Street (2006) sees as one of the obstacles to the viability of the social model of literacy.

A third explanation which has not been so explicitly acknowledged is the proximal relationship between the dominant autonomous model and the recognised measures of economic and production output. As acknowledged by Gee (2010), 'Dominant Discourses bring with it the potential acquisition of social goods, whereas non-dominant Discourses bring solidarity with a particular social network'. In my view, the major instrument for forging this proximal relationship is the curriculum. Because the curriculum offered by the autonomous model comes with the feature of 'quantifiability', as manifested in achievement levels which are driven by assessments such as the recent OECD-promoted PIAAC survey, it is easy to associate it with measurements of economic production, rightly or wrongly. Perhaps in acknowledgement of this relationship, Beauregard (2009) writes:

> Economically-motivated adult literacy education policies have altered the nature and purpose of adult literacy programs. Government intrusion into adult education has forced both individuals and community-based providers to relinquish their decision-making authority. In addition, government-imposed expectations and accountability requirements often supersede the individual learners' power to set their own goals.

The challenge for the proponents of alternative and non-autonomous models, therefore, is how to provide instruments that can enhance the ability of their model to measure productivity in a similar way. This does not necessarily imply an ideological selling out. Indeed, as noted by Brandt and Clinton (2002), proponents of the New Literacy Studies (NLS) ought to be more prepared to embrace some of the features of the dominant model (at least in its procedural form) without necessarily succumbing to the weaknesses of the model. My response to this, therefore, is to offer a social model of literacy curriculum development which I have labelled literacy for specific purposes (LSP) and which I shall explore below.

## Literacy for specific purposes: definition, underpinning principles and justifications

I use the term 'literacy for specific purposes' to define a literacy curriculum that is constructed to meet the needs of learners. In this sense, LSP is constructed in such a way that it is focused on the actual social, academic, professional and vocational needs of different learners. Within its framework, it is proposed that curricula should be designed around specific professional and vocational disciplines. In essence, LSP adopts a disciplinary model for curriculum design and, to use the specific language of the proponents of a social model of literacy, it is an approach to the construction of curricula around specific social practices.

The notion of specificity is not entirely new in the field of literacy. Indeed, several scholars in the field have engaged with specific literacies in one form or another. I shall briefly explore two of these contributions below. Recently, Mary Hamilton (2013) talked about what she classifies as 'the power of numbers' in literacy. She highlights the emergence of a particular literacy which uses numbers to disguise policy intention. To understand and use this literacy appropriately, she argues that one would need a full understanding of the social semiotic systems through which such texts are generated and understood. Drawing from the work of O'Halloran (2008) she shows how 'mathematical symbolism evolved from language to develop new grammatical systems of meaning so that precise description and manipulation of continuous patterns of relations between entities in time and space became possible'. In order to engage with texts in which such precise descriptions and manipulations are prominent, therefore, the reader needs a measure of proficiency in that specific form of literacy.

A second illustration of the specific nature of literacy is in the area of digital technology. One useful reference in this context is to the work of Guy Merchant. In many of his contributions, Merchant argues that 'literacy teaching and learning need to change because the world is changing' (Cope & Kalantzis, 2000, p. 41). This change involves new kinds of communicative relationships amongst students and between students and their teachers. In this sense, 'digital literacy can have a destabilising effect on traditional classroom routines' (Merchant, 2009:38). He argues that with the world changing in line with emerging technologies, it is inevitable that literacies would change too and, as a result, we would need to look at specific natures of the literacies we offer if we want to engage with this changing world. In effect, we must begin to consider the specific natures of the literacies we can offer.

My proposal in this chapter, however, goes a step further. To my mind, these illustrations are mostly descriptive in that they seem to identify elements that reflect the specific nature of different literacies. Responding to this is of course easy if the literacy in question is sufficiently elitist and acceptable to policy makers. For example, it seems easy to talk about digital literacy in classrooms as its essence converges with the government's vision to bring IT into the classroom. The ease with which this can be integrated into conventional models of schooling makes it acceptable. The issue arises when the specific literacy in question is not couched in such elitist status. What would be the response to specific literacies that are required and or demanded by less conventional learners such as the ones we gleefully refer to as 'NEETS'. This, in my view, is where the model of literacy curriculum for specific purposes comes in to play.

One work that appears to have bought into the notion of literacy for specific purposes that I advocate here is that of Hirsch (1988) on what he calls 'cultural literacy'. Before looking at the argument of Hirsch, let me state quickly that the convergence of my idea with that proposed by Hirsch is limited by the product of his vision of specificity in literacy curriculum. Although both Hirsch and I are agreed on the concept of developing specific literacy curricula, we differ on our views of what curricula should be specifically produced. Hirsch puts forward the notion of what strikes me as an elitist campaign for developing a specific cultural literacy which is identified by some elitist group with little recourse to the learners. By contrast, I argue that the specific nature of the curricula to be developed must be informed by the needs and goals of the learners and the discipline within which they desire to work.

Hirsch (1988) offers an educational theory which challenges Dewey's argument for a content-neutral conception of education. He concludes, 'Only by piling up specific, communally shared information can children learn to participate in complex cooperative activities' and that 'all human communities are founded upon specific shared information' (p. xv). While I share with the logic of specific shared information with Hirsch, the goal and the driver for my own LSP is markedly different. Specific literacies must be informed by what the learners of such literacies desire and should not be designed through a perception of what is perceived by others as desirable for learners to acquire. In this context, therefore, the learner is at the heart of the LSP I propose. The implication is that, unlike Hirsch, I do not propose a singular LSP, but in line with the principle of multi literacies, I suggest a concept of multiple LSPs.

## Underpinning principles of LSP

Underpinning the proposal for a LSP curriculum model are four key principles of social literacy (Barton, Hamilton 2000 & Ivanič, 2000) which have been modified to function as the foundation for LSP.

1   Barton and Hamilton contend that literacy is best understood as a set of social practices: literacy learning for adults is best constructed around practices which can manifest in disciplines, professions and vocations. Disciplinary vocations and professions are social practices and each has its own events that are peculiar to the discipline.
2   There are different literacies associated with different domains of life: there are different literacies associated with different disciplines, professions and vocations.
3   Literacy practices are purposeful and embedded in broader social goals and cultural practices: literacy practices can be purposeful and can be embedded in specific disciplinary and professional practices, each of which has its own literacy culture and norm.
4   Literacy practices change and new ones are frequently acquired through processes of informal learning and sense making: literacy needs in disciplinary areas will evolve as practices in the disciplines evolve and the literacy used by practitioners in different disciplines will keep pace with this evolution.

## Some cross-disciplinary theorization of LSP

The notion of developing LSP curricula argues for the development of literacy curricula, which acknowledges the professional and vocational preferences of learners in the expectation that such learners will be more engaged with literacy curricula that are designed with a focus on their own vocational goals. Using this model in the construction of literacy draws its justifications from pre-existing theories of English for Specific Purposes (ESP), register, langue and parole in the field of linguistics and Hirst's (1974) disciplinary theory.

## ESP and LSP

In my construction of LSP, I draw significantly from the theorisation of the existing cognate field of English for Specific Purposes (ESP). In contradistinction to general English, ESP focuses more on the learners and their purposes for learning English. ESP students are usually adults who already have some acquaintance with English and are learning the language in order to communicate a set of professional skills and to perform particular job-related functions. By the same token, I offer LSP as a model of curriculum design in the field of literacy which acknowledges the concepts of multi-literacies and multi-discourses emphasised by the proponents of the social model of literacy. In this regard, I argue that most adults and young people who are often conscripted into generic literacy classes already have one form of literacy, even if this form is merely what some would dismiss as mere orality (Street, 1995).

LSP, therefore, advocates for literacy curricula that are more focused on literacy in context rather than on generic structures. The central principle of LSP is that literacy for adults and alienated young people is neither designed nor taught as a subject separated from the students' real world and desires. Rather, it is integrated into a subject matter area important to the learners. A summary of what LSP is about is therefore constructed around the focus of ESP as offered in Strevens (1988) and Dudley-Evans (1998). An LSP curriculum must be designed to: meet specific needs of the learners in their quest for engagement with the reality of their preferred vocation; must therefore draw on the literacy related needs and activities of the discipline it serves and as is the case with ESP; and must seek to develop the language appropriate to these activities in terms of grammar, lexis, register, study skills, discourse and genre. Ironically, various initiatives in the UK, such as the recent Functional Skills initiative and the now defunct Key Skills initiatives, have borrowed from this principle. The problem, however, is with the targets of these initiatives. Both these initiatives are targeted at young learners who are already fully engaged in one form of study or the other. The gap is in how these initiatives could be applied to learners who are not engaged with any form of study largely because they are not considered to have the required levels of literacy and are not willing to engage with any form of generic literacy which they consider irrelevant. It is for this group of learners in particular that I propose LSP.

## The register theory and LSP

At the heart of the register theory (Eggins, 2004; Halliday & Hassan, 1989) is the notion that language varies according to the situation in which it is used. It is these varieties of usage that are referred to as registers. If we examine a text we can make guesses about the situation, on the other hand, if we are in a particular situation we make certain linguistic choices based on that situation. In other words, the language we use needs to be appropriate to the situation in which we use it. Drawing from this, therefore, we can offer a justification for arguing that the literacy we use must also be appropriate for the situation and that each situation requires specific literacies. This is one rationale for the proposal of LSP.

## Langue and parole and LSP

Similarly, Saussure (1916) draws a distinction between what he calls 'langue' and 'parole'. Whereas the former is the shared social structure of language and is richly structured as a system of systems, the latter is in the realm of the individual moments of language use (Van Lier, 2004; Heath, 1988). This distinction underpins the acknowledgement of literacy practices and events in the framework of the social model of literacy. In effect, there are different ways in which we use language for different purposes although the different uses, paroles, might all draw from the same source, langue. If we acknowledged the existence of different paroles, therefore, it is logical to anticipate the existence of different literacies, which is already acknowledged through the concept of multi-literacies (Anstey & Bull, 2006). What LSP aims to do is to take this to the next step, going beyond mere recognition of these literacies to facilitating their acquisition.

## The disciplinary thesis and LSP

A final theoretical anchor for the concept of a LSP curriculum draws from Hirst's (1973) notion of disciplinary studies. Though often criticised (Carr, 2004, 2005, 2006; Misawa, 2013), there is no doubt that there is some merit in Hirst's claim that education should be classified into classical liberal disciplines. As Hirst later writes (1996), the goal of the adventure into disciplinary classification of education was 'necessary to initiate them into the achievements of reason in knowledge and understanding and to promote the application of such knowledge in all areas of experience and action (p. 167). As Misawa (2013: 23) sees it, the relevance of Hirst's disciplinary thesis lies in his advocacy for a 'broad sense of education to initiate human animals into our world or the world of second nature filled with the meanings and humanly-perceived states of affairs that would otherwise make no sense'. This, in my view is what LSP can achieve. There are different worlds, or more aptly put, social practices for which we need specific literacies to understand and operate. Accepting this position naturally implies recognition of the need for and importance of a model of LSP. This is how we can most easily understand and promote the application of literacy in all areas of experience and action.

## Benefits of LSP: the Cultural Historical Activity Theory (CHAT) and constructionist explanations

What then might be the benefits of utilising an LSP model to curriculum development? First, because the basis of this model of literacy curriculum development, as I pointed out earlier, is the learner, a crucial benefit is the engagement of learners. Such an engagement derives from a crucial link between the learner's goal and the activities presented through LSP. To explain the crucial relationship between learner engagement and the use of LSP, I draw on the three basic models of Cultural Historical Activity Theory (CHAT) (Engestrom, 2001; Leont'ev, 1981; Nygard, 2013; Vygotsky, 1981). CHAT emphasises that the interaction of the subject with the world in which it exists ultimately leads to a situation in which there occurs 'mutual transformations between the poles of subject-object' (Leont'ev, 1981:31). CHAT identifies three crucial elements in the learning/developmental process: the subject, the object and the activity. It goes further to suggest that the 'subject and the object cannot be understood separately' (Nygard, 2013). In this context, the object is the goal, which represents what the activity is directed at. In the context of our disengaged and alienated literacy learners, the object would be their desired goal, which in many cases is a vocational endeavour. The subject, on the other hand, is the learner while the activity would be the curriculum and the ways in which it is delivered. In other words, the transformation of a learner will not occur unless there is an interaction between the learner and the world in which they learn. LSP simulates the world the learner desires and is, therefore, appropriately placed to stimulate that interaction. CHAT, therefore, shows the importance of the convergence between 'the outcome of the activity systems' which 'represents the goal of the activity and the object of the activity system' (Yasukawa, Brown & Black, 2013:3). Drawing from Engeström's (1999, 2001) postulations on CHAT, one can suggest that the learner in an LSP class, who as we have earlier argued is more interested in particular vocations, is a member of a specialised literacy community that 'establishes or at least subscribes to certain rules or ways' of using literacy 'that have become formally or informally accepted' in such a vocational or professional area. In other words, the learners' engagement with the LSP learning process is informed by the perception on the part of the learner that LSP is itself an activity system that can lead to the realisation of their own goals and objects. Furthermore, LSP learning for these students would amount to an element of belonging to a group with which they genuinely aspire to associate. As noted by Yasukawa et. al. (2013:4), what Engeström's schema offers in the analysis of engagement with concepts and processes is 'a way of understanding resistance and/or impetus for change in the established practices of the community'. In essence, a CHAT analysis shows us how and why these learners had not engaged with the cognitive model of literacy because of the divergence between the focus of that model of literacy and their own object and goals. Hence, there has been limited fluidity in the activity systems build around literacy learning for this group of learners.

### A constructionist explanation

A second driver for learner engagement through the use of LSP draws from the learning theory of constructionism (Papert 1980; Papert & Harel, 1991). Papert argues that, while learning from the view point of constructionism amounts to:

> building knowledge structures 'through progressive internalization of actions' . . . this happens especially felicitously in a context where the learner is consciously engaged in constructing a public entity, whether it's a sand castle on the beach or a theory of the universe.
>
> (1991:1)

In her acknowledgement of the arguments imbued in the constructionist theory of learning, Ackerman (2001) observes that

> because of its greater focus on learning through making rather than overall cognitive potentials, Papert's approach helps us understand how ideas get formed and transformed when expressed through different media, when actualized in particular contexts, when worked out by individual minds. The emphasis shifts from universals to individual learners' conversation with their own favourite representations, artefacts, or objects-to-think with.
>
> (p.438)

The relevance of this perception of learning for LSP is the convergence of perceptions between the two in two specific respects as illustrated below.

First, there is a move away from 'universals' and the opportunity for learners to develop 'conversations with their own favourite representations'. The construct of LSP offers hitherto disengaged learners an abundance of opportunities to generate conversations with their desired goals. As such, it is logical to expect a higher level of engagement with learning when these opportunities to develop preferred conversations are offered. A young literacy learner whose goal is, for example, to become a carpenter, will be more engaged with a literacy curriculum that is specifically focused on the literacy of carpentry than they would be if the curriculum were neutral and context free. The capacity to offer such opportunities, in my view, would encourage learners to become more engaged with literacy learning. This underscores another dimension in which LSP can be of benefit to learners who are generally condemned as disengaged or unable/unwilling to acquire literacy skills.

Second, there is a convergence between LSP and constructionism in the context of both principles' acknowledgement of the importance of the efficacy of learning through 'internalisation of action'. By its very nature, LSP is designed to focus on literacy skills leading to the development of vocational objectives. As such, it can be anticipated that such a focus will offer learners the opportunity to become involved in the process of constructing or at least, interacting with reality. Such opportunities, we argue, are bound to further the course of internalisation of action and, therefore, the engagement with, and promotion of, learning through the promotion of the integration of the vocational and cognitive worlds.

Insights from both CHAT and constructionism, as presented above, help to concretise the argument that LSP has the potential to be of benefit to disengaged learners. Central to this argument is the issue of engagement. Too often practitioners and policy makers have decried the lack of engagement of young people with literacy problems. The argument of LSP is that many of these learners are disengaged because the literacy curriculum they are offered neither enables them to construct the reality dictated by their goals, nor does it offer activities that predict a convergence between the learners' and the curricula's objects. What LSP has the potential to do is to create a learning construct which not only enables these learners to construct their own desired reality but also create a series of activities which share a similar object as those of the learners. Effecting these two goals is more likely to promote learner engagement.

## Some challenges to the implementation of LSP

As with most innovations, there are bound to be challenges to be faced with this call for a new way of developing literacy curriculum. In this section, I present two of those challenges which I suggest might be the most difficult to surmount. The first major challenge is intrinsic to the LSP thesis itself and this revolves around the process for mapping out disciplinary boundaries. How do we map out the various disciplines around which LSP curricula are to be built? This is important because current, education-based debates have questioned the assumption 'that there is a corpus of disciplinary received wisdom that is beyond criticism' (Kelly, Luke & Green, 2008; Venville, Rennie & Curtin Wallace 2009:1). Some of the apprehensions expressed in these debates are anchored on the argument that disciplinary knowledge might, in the words of Venville et al. (2009:1), ultimately 'be translated in curriculum documents throughout the world into key criteria, standards, or educational outcomes that are narrowly focused on what is readily measurable, or amenable to standardized achievement testing'. They argue that in the pursuit of disciplinary curricula 'there is a real risk of reducing the opportunities for students to engage in more contextual, issue-based and applied learning that does not fit within the boundaries of the traditional disciplines'. This, obviously, will be antithetical to the goals of LSP. The challenge, therefore, is how we pursue the development of LSP without unwittingly falling into the danger of creating robotic standard driven curricula which have the potential of stifling the creativity of learners.

The second challenge that can be predicted with LSP is the cost of curriculum development. There is no doubt that embracing this approach will have attendant cost implications both in terms of curriculum and expertise development. As illustrated by Savin-Baden (2003: 338) in the context of the development of curricula for problem-based learning, there is 'unplanned-for, long-term cost' associated with such innovations. Associated with the issue of cost is the challenge of acceptability to policy makers who will provide funding and other relevant agencies such as awarding bodies who are well positioned to give such a development a seal of approval and legitimacy. These are issues that must be confronted and surmounted if LSP is to fully achieve its potential.

## References

Ackermann, E. (2001) 'Piaget's constructivism, Papert's constructionism: What's the difference?' *Future of learning group publication*, 5(3): 438.

Anstey, M. and Bull, G. (2006) 'Responding to rapid change: multiliteracies and ICT', in EQ Australia, Curriculum Corporation, Winter, pp. 17–18.

Beauregard, H. (2009) 'The evolution of adult literacy education policy in the United States and the erosion of student-empowered learning'. MEd/Ed.D Dissertation, Ohio State University. Available online from: https://etd.ohiolink.edu/ap:10:0::NO:10:P10_ETD_SUBID:68862 (last accessed 1 September 2014).

Brandt, D. and Clinton, K. (2002) 'Limits of the local: Expanding perspectives on literacy as a social practice', *Journal of Literacy Research*, 34(3): 337–356.

Carr, W. (2004) 'Philosophy and education', *Journal of Philosophy of Education*, 38(1): 55–73.

Carr, W. (2005) 'What is the philosophy of education?' in Carr, W. (ed) *The Routledge Falmer reader in the philosophy of education*. London: Routledge, pp. 1–14.

Carr, W. (2006) 'Education without theory', *British Journal of Educational Studies*, 54(2): 136–59.

Collins, J. and Blot, R. K. (2003) *Literacy and literacies: text, power and identity*. Cambridge: Cambridge University Press.

Cope, B. & Kalantzis, M. (eds) (2000) *Mulitliteracies: Literacy learning and the design of social futures*. South Yarra: Macmillan.

Cornbleth, C. (1990) *Curriculum in context*. Basingstoke: Falmer Press.

Cornbleth, C. (2000) *Curriculum politics, policy, practice: cases in comparative context*. New York: State University of New York Press.

Duckworth, V. (2013) *Learning trajectories, violence and empowerment amongst adult basic skills learners*. London: Routledge.

Dudley-Evans, T. (1998) *Developments in English for specific purposes: a multi-disciplinary approach*. Cambridge: Cambridge University Press.

Eggins, S. (2004) *An introduction to systemic functional linguistics*, 2nd edition, New York/London: Continuum.

Engeström, Y. (1999) 'Innovative learning in work teams: analysing cycles of knowledge creation in practice'. In Engeström, Y., Miettimem, R. & Punamäki, R.-L. (eds.) *Perspectives on activity theory*, Cambridge: Cambridge University Press, pp. 377–406.

Engeström, Y. (2001) 'Expansive learning at work: toward an activity theoretical reconceptualization', *Journal of Education and Work*, 14: 133–156.

Fiorito, L. (2005) Teaching English for Specific Purposes. Retrieved online from:  www. usingenglish.com/articles/teaching-english-for-specific-purposes-esp.html (last accessed 21 August 2014).

Gee, J. P. (2001) 'Literacy, discourse, and linguistics: introduction and what is literacy?' in Cushman, E., Kintgen, E. R., Knoll, B. M. & Rose, M. (eds) *Literacy: a critical sourcebook*. New York: Bedford, pp. 525-544.

Gee, J. (2010) *An introduction to discourse analysis*. London: Taylor and Francis.

Grundy, S. (1987) *Curriculum: product or praxis*. Lewes: Falmer.

Halliday, M. A. K. & Hasan, R. (1989) *Language, context, and text: aspects of language in a social semiotic perspective*. Oxford: Oxford University Press.

Hamilton, M. (2013) 'Literacy and the power of numbers'. Paper presented at Institute of Education CeCeps Seminar Series, 24 January 2013.

Heath, S. (1988) 'Translator's note' in Barthes, R. *Image music text*. London: Macmillan.

Hirsch, E. D. (1998) *Cultural literacy: what every american needs to know*. Vintage Books: New York.

Hirst, P. H. (1973) 'Liberal education and the nature of knowledge' in: Peters, R. S. (ed.) *The philosophy of education: Oxford readings in philosophy*. London: Oxford University Press, pp. 87–111.

Hirst, P. H. (1974) *Knowledge and the curriculum*. London: Routledge and Kegan Paul.

Hirst, P. H. (1993) 'Education, knowledge and practices' in Barrow, B. & White, P. (eds) *Beyond liberal education: essays in honour of Paul H. Hirst*. London: Routledge, pp. 184–99.

Hirst, P. H. (1996) 'The demands of professional practice and preparation for teaching' in Furlong, J. & Smith, R. (eds) *The role of higher education in initial teacher training*. London: Kogan Page, pp. 166–78.

Hirst, P. H. (1999) 'The nature of educational aims' in Marples, R. (ed.) *The aims of education. Routledge international studies in the philosophy of education, 7*. London: Routledge, pp. 124–32.

Hirst, P. H. (2008) 'In pursuit of reason' in Waks, L. J. (ed.) *Leaders in philosophy of education: intellectual self portrait*. Rotterdam: Sense, pp. 1–13.

Hirst, P. H. & Carr, W. (2005) 'Philosophy and education: a symposium', *Journal of Philosophy of Education*, 39(4): 615–32.

Hirst, P. H. & White. P. (1998) 'The analytic tradition and philosophy of education: an historical perspective' in Hirst, P. H .& White. P. (eds) *Philosophy of education major themes in the analytic tradition. Volume I, philosophy and education*. London: Routledge, pp. 1–12.

Hutchinson, T. & Waters, A. (1987). *English for specific purposes: A learner-centered approach*. Cambridge: Cambridge University Press.

Jeffs, T. J. & Smith, M. (eds.) (1990) *Using informal education. an alternative to casework, teaching and control?* Milton Keynes: Open University Press.

Jeffs, T. J. and Smith, M. K. (1999) *Informal education. conversation, democracy and learning*. Ticknall, UK: Education Now.

Johns, A. M. & Dudley-Evans, T. (1991). 'English for specific purposes: international in scope, specific in purpose', *TESOL Quarterly* 25(2): 297–314.

Kelly, G. J., Luke, A., & Green, J. (eds) (2008). 'What counts as knowledge in educational settings: disciplinary knowledge, assessment, and curriculum', *Review of Research in Education*, 3(32): 292–327.

Larson, J. (2000) 'Challenging autonomous models of literacy: Street's call to action', *Linguistics and Education*, 8(4): 439–45.

Leont'ev, A. N. (1981). *Problems of the development of the mind*. Moscow: Progress Publishers.

Merchant, G. (2009) 'Literacy in virtual worlds', *Journal of Research in Reading*, 32(1): 38–56.

Misawa, K. (2013) 'The Hirst-Carr debate revisited: beyond the theory-practice dichotomy', *Journal of Philosophy of Education*, 45(4): 689–702.

Nygard, K. (2013) Cultural Historical Activity Theory (CHAT) TOOL 5100/ INF 5200. Accessed online from: http://www.uio.no/studier/emner/matnat/ifi/TOOL5100/v08/foiler/F4-CHAT-120208.pdf on (last accessed 14 December 2013).

OECD (2010) *The OECD programme for the international assessment of adult competencies (PIAAC)*, Paris: OECD Publications.

OECD News Room (2013a) 'Better policies for better lives: "boosting skills essential for tackling joblessness and improving well-being"'. Retrieved online from: http://www.oecd.org/newsroom/boosting-skills-essential-for-tackling-joblessness-and-improving-well-being.htm (last accessed 16 October 2013).

OECD News Room (2013b) 'Better policies for better lives: "innovations in education: adult literacy"'. Retrieved online from: http://www.oecd.org/newsroom/boosting-skills-essential-for-tackling-joblessness-and-improving-well-being.htm (last accessed 16 October 2013).

O'Halloran, K. L. (2008) 'Systemic Functional-Multimodal Discourse Analysis (SF-MDA): constructing ideational meaning using language and visual imagery', *Visual Communication* 7(4): 443-475.

Papert, S. (1980). *Mindstorms: children, computers and powerful ideas*. New York: Basic Books.

Papert, S. & Harel, I. (1991) 'Situating constructionism'. In *Constructionism: Research reports and essays*. New York: Ablex Publishing Corporation.

Saussure, F. (1916) *Course in General Linguistics*. Reconstructed posthumously by his students, Referred to in this work through Richard L. W. Clarke LITS3304 2009-2010 Notes 01, Retrieved online from: http://www.rlwclarke.net/courses/LITS3304/2009-2010/01SaussureOverview.pdf (last accessed 20 August 2013).

Savin-Baden, M. (2003) 'Problem-based learning disciplinary differences or modes of curriculum practice?' *Biochemistry and Molecular Biology Education*, 31(5): 338–43.

Stenhouse, L. (1975) *An introduction to curriculum research and development*. London: Heinemann.

Street, B. (1995) *Social literacies: critical approaches to literacy in development, ethnography and education*. London: Longman.

Street, B. (2005) Applying New Literacy Studies to numeracy as social practice' in *Urban literacy: communication, identity and learning in development contexts*. Hamburg: UNESCO Institute for Education, pp. 87–96.

Street, B. (2012) 'Society reschooling', *Reading Research Quarterly* 47(2): 216–227.

Strevens, P. (1988). 'ESP after twenty years: a re-appraisal' in Tickoo, M. (ed.) *ESP: state of the art*. Singapore: SAMEO Regional Language Centre, pp. 1–13.

Van Lier, L. (2004) *The ecology and semiotics of language learning: a sociocultural perspective*. Berlin: Birkhäuser.

Venville, G., Rennie, L. & Curtin Wallace, J. (2009) 'Disciplinary versus integrated curriculum', *The New Critic*, 10: August 2009. Retrieved online from: http://www.ias.uwa.edu.au/new-critic (last accessed 20 August 2013).

Vygotsky, L. S. (1981) 'The genesis of higher mental functions'. In Wertsch, J. V. (ed.) *The concept of activity in Soviet psychology*. Armonk: Sharpe.

Whitehead, J. (1999) 'Educative relations in a new era', *Pedagogy, Culture & Society*, 7(1): 73–90.

Yasukawa, K., Brown, T. & Black, S. (2012) Exploring Cultural-Historical Activity Theory (CHAT) as a tool for investigating workers' literacy and numeracy practices. Paper presented at the15th Annual AVETRA Conference, Canberra, April 2012. Accessed online from http://avetra.org.au/wp-content/uploads/2012/05/Paper-69-Yasukawa-Brown-Black-final1.pdf (last accessed 19 December 2013).

# Chapter 3

# Literacy and transformation

*Vicky Duckworth*

## Introduction

This chapter draws on the findings of my recent longitudinal ethnographic study which explored how sixteen learners have been shaped, their whole being influenced by and responding to, the public domain of schooling, college and work and the private domain of family, friends and home. The aim was to explore the learners' perceptions of their reality in these domains whilst seeking to address in what ways their past, present and future have been influenced by class and gender and how this has impacted on their pathways and subsequent trajectories (Duckworth 2013). The learners were all enrolled on either a part-time or full-time Adult Basic Skills course at a Further Education College based in the north of England. I was their literacy teacher and the drive to partake in the study came from my experience of living and working with learners from disadvantaged backgrounds. I felt that the notion of neo-liberalism and its implication that an individual is free to determine their own pathway, is limited by the impact of structural and historical inequalities: gender, race and class and other markers of identity that shape the learners' educational journeys (Leathwood 2006). One way in which this happens is that learners from disadvantaged backgrounds are not considered to have the right attributes to progress (Archer et al. 2003; Burke 2006; Duckworth and Cochrane 2012). As a critical educator/researcher, my aim was to challenge a hegemonic[1] curriculum and instead open a meaningful 'space' to reflect a critical pedagogy, providing a curriculum which is culturally relevant, learner driven and socially empowering (Barton et al. 2007; Duckworth 2010, 2013; Duckworth and Taylor 2008; Duckworth and Tummons 2014; Freire 1996; Hamilton 2012).

## Overview of adult literacy

Adult literacy has a long history, but has particularly grown in prominence during the last three decades. In conjunction with post-compulsory education and training (PCET), it has been significantly reshaped by national policy initiatives since the 1970s when the government took a bigger interest in the education and training of adults, as the concept of lifelong learning fed into international policy documents (Field 2000).

The mid 1970s saw a literacy campaign led by a coalition of voluntary agencies and partnered with the media, namely the British Broadcasting Corporation (BBC). The 'Right to Read' movement, which emerged in the 1970s as a grassroots campaign, went on to receive national government funding and to develop into a national unit – the Adult Literacy Resource Agency, which later became the Basic Skills Agency – briefed with the task of pushing forward adult literacy provision (Hamilton 1996). This period saw a considerable development of basic skills, supported by the Local Education Authority (LEA) Adult Education Services and voluntary organisations, with leadership, training and development funding from a national agency – the Adult Literacy and Basic Skills Agency (ALBSU), later the Basic Skills Agency (BSA).

By the 1990s there was a reduction in LEA funding and control. Instead, basic skills were given statutory status through a more formal further education (FE) system which was dependent on funding through a national funding body – the Further Education Funding Council (FEFC) (see Hamilton and Hillier 2006). The late 1990s also saw 'A Fresh Start – Improving Literacy and Numeracy' produced by a working group chaired by Sir Claus Moser. This helped shape the Labour government's strategy to improve the literacy, language and numeracy (LLN) skills of adults (DfEE 1999). The report recommended that a national strategy for adult basic skills be developed to begin to address literacy and numeracy skills needs. It had aspiring targets for reducing the number of adults with low skills levels. The Moser Report pulled on some of the evidence in the survey to estimate that approximately 20 per cent of the UK population (as many as seven million people) apparently had difficulty with functional literacy and/or numeracy. This was defined as 'the ability to read, write and speak in English and use mathematics at a level necessary to function at work and in society in general'. The resulting strategy, *Skills for Life* (*SfL*), identified a number of priority groups which included people who live in disadvantaged communities (DfEE 2001).

In this changing landscape adult literacy and numeracy provision is now a recognised component of vocational education and training in the United Kingdom. The politics of curriculum, including LLN, is a key issue for policy makers, researchers, managers and practitioners. Indeed, the model of curriculum can determine whether education is an emancipating or suppressing process. Therefore, the lifelong curriculum, which includes *SfL*, may be situated not as neutral or apolitical but at the centre of educational power. For example, in an age of globalisation and neoliberalism it may be viewed as a product of market driven changes, where approaches to *SfL* involve a functional literacy approach. This is defined by its social purposes, in which there is an alignment between individual skills, the performance of society, the global economy and economic productivity. Easily testable outcomes, such as the *SfL* end tests, are often what the lifelong learning sector follows to measure performance, pull down funding and beat national benchmarks. Deficits are measured against a fixed and discrete set of transferable skills. What it fails to recognise and address is the historical and contemporary disparities that exist in the structural inequalities between the learners and their lives e.g. class, gender and ethnicity. The implications of this are that the meaningful literacy practices that a community of learners bring with them, which are historically and socially constituted based on their backgrounds and experiences, are not given value in the classroom.

The dominant model of delivering literacies has a strong utilitarian function, which selects and distributes literacy in different ways to different social groups, reproducing class inequalities which fail to address issues of power relations in the learners' lives (see Crowther et al. 2006). This market driven model often fails to recognise literacy as a tool for personal enlightenment. Gee argues that a way to address structural inequalities which disadvantage children is to:

> fight the neo-liberal agenda and make schools sites for creativity, deep thinking, and the formation of whole people: sites in which all children can gain portfolios for success defined in multiple ways, and gain the ability to critique and transform social formations in the service of creating better worlds for all.

> (2004:110)

I suggest that a way to challenge an instrumental curriculum is to move towards a *caring, critical, co-construction model* (CCCM) based on a social approach. Social approaches to literacy are sometimes grouped together under the remit of the New Literacy Studies (Barton 1994; Barton and Hamilton 1998; Gee 1996; Street 1984). Within this complex view of the nature of literacy we can highlight that literacy has many purposes for the learner. It challenges the dominance of the autonomous model, and recognises how literacy practices vary from one cultural and historical context to another. For example, in the private domain of home and public domain of formal education, literacy practices, identities and discourse are produced by power and ideology so that literacy is shaped differently in different contexts. This focus can support tutors to shift from a narrow competency-based approach, which separates the literacies from their context and instead harness the everyday practices learners bring into the classroom. As such, literacy is not just a technical or neutral skill, it provides a social view which is expanded by considering literacy as not only a social practice but also as a multimodal form of communication. It recognises music, images, symbols and other forms as being literacy practices. The use of multi-modal literacies offers the expansion of the ways learners acquire information and understand concepts (Duckworth and Brzeski forthcoming). This approach moves from a deficit model of literacies, and instead recognises that 'language, literacy and numeracy involves paying attention first and foremost to the contexts, purposes and practices in which language (spoken and written) and mathematical operations play a part (Barton et al. 2007:17).

In addition to NLS, I also draw on Freire (1996) who addresses who and what education is for and whose group interests are promoted. He examines the ideologies of classroom practice and, in his challenge to the 'banking' system, recommends a critical pedagogy model for teaching adult literacy. Educationalist theorists have developed this approach (see Duckworth 2013; Giroux 1997; Lankshear 1993; Lankshear and McLaren 1992; Shor 1992, 1993). They have challenged prescriptive approaches to curriculum designs which do not take into account the history or background and needs of learners. These non-critical curriculums place dominance on an instrumental approach ignoring the political, social and economic factors that have conspired to marginalise the learners and the communities they live in. Having been born, brought up and living in the emotional and geographical landscape of the learners, I am immersed in their communities. This immersion allowed me, as a practitioner, a critical positioning whereby I have insider knowledge of their lives, motivations, pressures, hopes and dreams (see Giroux 1997; Macedo 1994; Shor 1992). It is from this position that the critical model moves towards the learner being the co-producer of knowledge. In doing so it shifts away from teacher-directed, top-down, commonly imposed and standardised assessments that prescribe the same for all students, regardless of their ability, values, ethnicity, history, their community requirements or their specific contexts. Instead it takes an egalitarian approach, whereby there is a sharing of power between the teacher and the student in learning, the curriculum, its contents and methods. Freire (1996) proposed to do this via 'culture circles'. A culture circle is a discussion group in which educators and learners use codifications to engage in dialectic engagement for consciousness raising, liberation, empowerment and transformation. Education for liberation provides a forum open to the empowerment of learners, teachers and the community, while also providing opportunities for the development of those skills and competencies without which empowerment would be impossible.

In order to develop these skills, linking with NLS offers a socially situated model which, like the Freirian culture circle, challenges dominant models of literacy, for example replacing the economic driven model associated with workforce training, productivity and the notion of human capital[2] (institutional literacies) with a socio-cultural model which includes vernacular literacies. It recognises that literacy practices are formed in a number of contexts and domains, for example the private domain of home and the public domain of schooling. In their book, *Local Literacies*, Barton and Hamilton (1998) explore the many literacy activities people are involved in across the different domains of their life. A key aspect of their findings is that people have 'ruling passions' which can be a key to where, why and what literacy practices mattered to them. As a tutor, knowledge of learners' ruling passions offers a means to recognise and celebrate the learners' practices. Whether the practice is drawing, words, poetry or photographs like the culture circles, NLS draws on the literacies from the learners' lives. These artefacts are a way to develop a dialogue leading to an analysis of the concrete reality represented by the learners and facilitating them to address inequalities in their lives.

## Identity and literacy

Papen (2005) argues that literacy and identity exist together. Indeed, Duckworth (2013) highlights that a personal level literacy lies in the development of self-identity, in our social, cultural and emotional life, happiness and wellbeing. Papen (2005:147) further explains that, as literacy is a social practice, then this commonly implies inclusion of the cultural, that is the values, ideas, conventions, worldviews and *identities* that shape the event of which literacy is a part. Therefore, identity is an integral part of, and an influencing factor upon, the literacy practice itself. For the male and female learners in this study, returning to education was a means for them to develop their literacy skills. Literacy was very much linked with their subjectivity and how they viewed their self-worth in the public and private domains of their lives. Barton and Hamilton (1998:170) suggest that people assert their identities *through* their literacy practices and can demarcate themselves, their partners and other members of their households in terms of literacy practices such as 'I usually read to the children and he buys the newspaper'. When considering the vernacular literacies the learners brought to the classroom, they were united in what Shirley Brice Heath (1983) describes as their 'way with words' which did not privilege their literacy practices at school or within the Lifelong Learning Sector (LLS). This influenced their experience at school, the 'choices' they had or did not have and subsequent trajectories as adults.

The literacies the learners brought into the classroom as working class children at school and as adults in further education, afforded little dominant symbolic value in that it could not be used in class to pass exams. For example, the domestic and caring literacy which has been traditionally carried out by girls and women seldom enters the public domain and often remains invisible and unrecognised. The working class practices, which were often gendered, were not valued. Wrapped in notions of literacies, were domination and symbolic violence. Oral and written linguistic capabilities were not equally valued in schools (or the workplace) and even within the oral tradition, the codes of the upper classes were prioritised over the codes of working class and ethnically diverse learners (Bernstein 1971b; Labov 1972). This inevitably meant that learners who were not proficient in the linguistic skills required in schools and colleges were defined as failures or lacking in intelligence simply by virtue of the way they relate to and know the world. As their teacher I looked for meaningful approaches and strategies to link with their 'way with words' and empower the learners to reach their goals.

## Theoretical overview

This study drew on Bourdieu's theory 'The forms of capital' (2001) as a framework, providing the tools for understanding how the learners' narrative accounts of their educational and personal journey from childhood to Basic Skills Learner and beyond have been shaped. Bourdieu explains the production of inequality within society by the forms of capital: economic capital, social capital, cultural capital and symbolic capital. Cultural capital can be broken down into three categories: 1) an embodied state of mind and body (see Reay 2005); 2) objectified and 3) institutionalised (see Bourdieu 2001). Bourdieu's theoretical framework and concepts enabled me to expose and explore the impact of structural determinants such as class and gender on the constraints and choices available to the learners on their trajectories. The concept of cultural capital was vital in exposing the transmission of wealth and power and incorporating ideas about how those in a position of power, who Puwar (2004) describes as 'insiders', reproduce and maintain their domination; whilst the concepts of habitus, field and symbolic domination helped me to better understand how mechanisms of power that enable inequalities are embodied in places, people, historical and social existences, and as such are difficult to remove. Drawing on the learners narratives, I identified features of symbolic capital/or the lack of it across the domains of their lives and the impact of this. Uncovering and understanding what are often invisible forms of symbolic capital and trying to understand how this impacts on the lives and the communities of the learners offered a valuable knowledge. Indeed drawing on the learners' narratives, I identified features of symbolic violence that are embedded in everyday life. This allowed me to explore the different forms of violence that can co-exist and indeed support one another, each impacting on the other in a cycle of violence. Critical education offered me the opportunity to extend on Bourdieu's concept by including this as a lever for challenging symbolic violence and offering the potential for learner empowerment and emancipation (Duckworth 2013).

## Research methodology

The research approach was based on strategies which include participatory action research (PAR) and feminist standpoint theory, whilst also drawing on life history, literacy studies and ethnographic approaches to exploring social practices. The drive was to provide the environment and tools to facilitate learners to celebrate their ways of knowing, rather than dominant models of what is considered legitimate knowledge (Barton and Hamilton 1998). There was a recognition of the vernacular literacies and other embodied knowledge that learners (and the teacher) bring into the classroom. In engaging in collaborative research, an aim was also to facilitate the participants to acquire the critical tools to transform their own lives. Indeed, praxis involves a dedication to challenging the status quo and helping people from marginalised communities understand their oppression, such as recognising structural inequalities of class, gender and ethnicity and through realisation, reflection and change, shift accountability of traumatised narratives from the pathologised self. For example, see Figure 3.1 which illustrates the impact of learners lack of linguistic capital on the symbolic and physical violence they experienced from teachers and peers.

PAR builds on critical pedagogy put forward by Freire as a response to the traditional formal models of education where the teacher takes the power and imparts information to the students that are passive empty vessels waiting to be filled. This model fails to recognise the powerful knowledge learners bring into the classroom with them, such as socially situated knowledge (see Barton and Hamilton 1998, Duckworth 2013). In this vein, the main goal of PAR is for both researcher/practitioner and participant to work in egalitarian ways and develop effective dialogue and critical consciousness and, in the case of this study, a critical curriculum which facilitates this. It was very important that the participants (learners) were involved in the research (and curriculum design) process, the goal of PAR being democratic, participatory, giving a voice to the

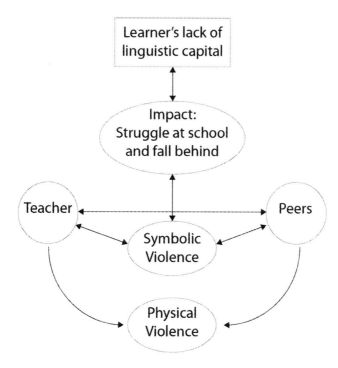

*Figure 3.1* Linguistic capital and the cycle of symbolic and physical violence by peers and teachers

oppressed. As such, the dialogical relationships between my teaching, research and learners led to continual changes in all three. This change and praxis flowed between the researcher/practitioner and learner as identified and described in Figure 3.2.

## The learners' journey into college

On arrival at college there was a strong feeling by the learners that, paralleling their experiences at school, they would be judged and pathologised by others for being poor and struggling with literacy. In our discussions there was a link between what they considered their 'poor' literacy skills and viewing themselves as childlike because of that. This is hardly surprising when in all aspects of society including entering learning, basic skills learners are labelled as lacking and in many case put to the bottom of the list when it comes to the hierarchy of employment and courses offered in college. Further to this, the dominant discourse that runs through adult education (like that of compulsory education) is often constructed on a deficit model which positions the learners as lacking in relation to what are widely deemed as the norms of literacy. Indeed, literacy is not simply about mastering a code but, within a dominant framework, about developing power over literacy practices that are recognised as 'legitimate', that is, situationally defined, arbitrarily sanctioned forms of reading or writing with legitimate audiences (Bourdieu 1991).

A key drive for the learners' commencing the literacy programmes was to become literate. The classes were also viewed as means to gain respectability and

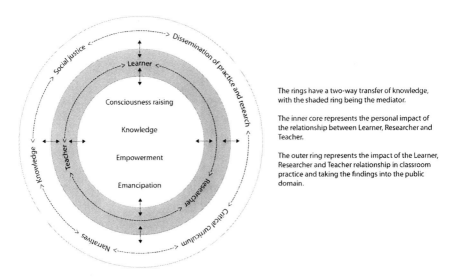

The rings have a two-way transfer of knowledge, with the shaded ring being the mediator.

The inner core represents the personal impact of the relationship between Learner, Researcher and Teacher.

The outer ring represents the impact of the Learner, Researcher and Teacher relationship in classroom practice and taking the findings into the public domain.

*Figure 3.2* Personal and public impact of PAR

what was considered normality. The development of literacy skills, confidence and self-esteem was linked to the learners seeing other possible choices in their lives. For many of the learners the adult literacy classes were their last hope of education.

## Joanne's story

Joanne left the local state school, at fifteen, without qualifications and used her practical know-how to work as a machinist out of necessity and the need to earn a wage. She said that: 'Machining summat I picked up really easy. It's not like yer need exams. It's summat most women can do.' The catalyst to Joanne returning to college was the breakup of her relationship. A single mother of three children, she arrived at college struggling to read and write and for the first few weeks sat at the back of the class. Avoiding eye contact, she hardly said a word, except to express her fear of writing owing to what she called 'rubbish spelling'. She described being labelled and pathologised by teachers as early as primary school for lacking the qualities deemed necessary to succeed (see Steedman 1988). Joanne was labelled because she was poor and came from a 'big family' the antithesis to a *respectable* 'nuclear family'. The idea of a big family, I would suggest, is linked to poverty, lack of restraint, sexuality, savage and as such pathologised. For Joanne coming from a big family and not 'aving nowt to buy new clothes' meant she was viewed as a 'scruff' and 'pushed to one side'

> If you come from big families you were just pushed to the side. I remember being really good at badminton, but cos I was a X . . . come from a big family I couldn't go on the team. Anyhow – we could do what we want the teachers weren't interested in the end. – It was cos we were the ones who stood out cos of our clothes. Yer know they're looking down on yer cos yer wearin' hand me downs. Yer feel dirty somehow, daft really cos all our clothes has been washed, they were old that's all. Yer can't wash the tattiness out I suppose.
>
> (Joanne)

On being asked why she was attending college, Joanne initially described how: 'I want to be able to fill in forms on me own and be more confident in me spelling'. Opening up a space for critical reflection and dialogue in class and in the research group both Joanne (and the other learners) challenged notions of what literacies are. It was this move from a competence-based model to a holistic approach (see Morrish et al. 2002) and care (see Feeley 2014) which was strengthened as a result of the PAR and the strong bonds formed with the learners that allowed a critical space for me to fully explore the learners' motivations and barriers. Both the approach of the research and the lessons also worked to encourage the learners to reflect. This was a tool for 'consciousness-raising' (Freire 1996) and praxis. The praxis was linked with social action and emancipation (see Figure 3.2). The critical spaces which were provided in the research and the class moved towards a deepened consciousness in which the learners, were able to recognise that they are products of history and as such challenge the structural conditions of oppression (see Freire 1996).

As Joanne's confidence increased in both herself and her writing skills, there was a simultaneous shift in aspirations, this was the first time she had planned for the future. She began to make choices that she previously thought were deemed as not for people from her background. She spoke about a career rather than a job, describing how: 'I want to be a good role model for my children, getting a career can give us all a better future'.

Joanne broke down the barriers that had held her back for so long and on her journey; successfully completed a level-two course in Literacy and Numeracy; progressed onto an Access to Nursing course and then to university. She passed her diploma and is now a qualified staff nurse working in the north of England.

Below, Joanne tells her story in her own words. This was part of the writing she shared with me when she began to explore writing her learning autobiography (see McNamara 2007):

Do you know three years ago if I had to fill in anything like a form I couldn't, it may as well have been written in another language. In the end I did not even bother looking at any forms that were sent to me. I would just go to my sister and ask her to fill them in for me and I would just sign them. There are so many other things that I could tell you about how not being able to read, write and spell has affected my life, but the chances are that if you're reading this you already know about most of them.

Through learning to read and write etc. I now see life differently. Now when my children bring homework home I'm right onto it. I sit down with them and we go through their work together. For example, my son X is only eight and he has 20 spellings a week to learn. This week he had words such as exhibition, examination and electrocution. Before returning to education I would never have been able to help him with words like this, so the chances are he would not have learnt them. He would have gone to school, had his spelling test. Maybe he got 4 or 5 out of 20, if he was lucky, felt a bit daft in front of the children who had got most [of] them right and slowly but surely before you know it, it's a knock on effect, history is repeating itself. But because I can now sit down with X and help him with his homework he gets marks like 17 out of 20, which to me is pretty amazing. I really feel that in my case because I'm all my children have, if I'd not have returned to education the chances are that my children would have ended up experiencing difficulties in their education. I'm not saying that they won't but if they do, like I did, I can now help them. In today's world qualifications are needed in most jobs, again proving how important learning is.

   . . . I just want to say that returning to education for me was one of the most frightening things that I have ever done, but one of the best. There have been times when I have wanted to quit because I found it too hard and believe me I have cried in frustration. There are two things that have kept me going, one is my beautiful children, they are depending on me and the other is my teacher, who is always on my case, only messing! She has been amazing. She is the one who when I've thought 'What's the point?' has kept me going. She made me believe that I can achieve my goal if I work hard enough and so far she has been right.

(Duckworth 2013)

The transformation of Joanne's aspirations and her life impacted on her children's progression and the transformation in the dynamics of the family. She no longer felt childlike but empowered to support her children. Their grades improved and Joanne felt much more confident and valued in her role as a mother. Joanne's behaviour and notion of motherhood has changed as her habitus has been shaped by the field of education (college and university) and job (nursing). This has resulted in higher expectation of the job her youngest children progress to.

Figure 3.3 illustrates the cycle of linguistic deprivation and disempowerment across the domain of family and demonstrates how resistance capital (this time after the break-up of a relationship) can be a trigger to commencing college and gaining linguistic and cultural capital as well as empowerment for Joanne and her family.

## Carol's story

When Carol, a single mother and grandmother in her fifties, started the evening basic skills class, like Joanne, she initially had no confidence in writing. Indeed, the idea of writing for creative expression was unthinkable. From the age of two and a half years old she was brought up in a convent, where schooling was not as high on the rota as cooking and cleaning. She did enjoy reading though, and would be mocked by the other girls as 'an old lady'. On leaving the convent at fifteen, with no qualifications or money in her pocket, she travelled to Dublin then across the waters to London before eventually settling in Oldham. In between bringing up three daughters, single-handedly, she continued to do mainly cleaning jobs. She described how the experience of growing up in a convent involved using caring and domestic capital. The transference of caring capital has been explored in the realm of adulthood (for example, see Feeley 2007; Luttrell 1997; Lynch et al. 2008; O'Brien 2005; Reay 2000), but rarely in the realm of childhood. The use of Carol's caring capital is particularly poignant as without a family, she lacked caring herself. Carol expressed that:

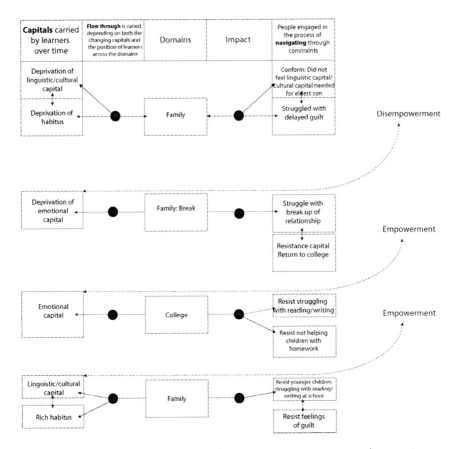

*Figure 3.3* Cycle of linguistic deprivation, disempowerment, resistance and supporting children to gain linguistic capital

> I got on well with the girls alright, because I was as daft as the younger ones but I knew if you were older than someone you looked after them, just sort of a mother figure you took over.

Carol also describes her domestic role in the convent: 'We all mucked into the cleaning. I took real pride in it, made sure I did it well'.

In the formal and informal interviews, Carol voiced how experiencing a childhood in care and a string of abusive relationships with 'no good' men had 'knocked away' her confidence. In and out of depression she wanted to 'do something with me brain'. Although occasionally daring to think about writing 'maybe poetry or summat', when she arrived on the course and I expressed how the class may cover topics which include poetry and story-telling, she seemed resigned that poetry was not for her. Carol firmly believed that only people who've 'got qualifications and yer know good jobs' can write poetry, 'they're the clever ones'. She described how she felt almost scared of exploring the possibilities of language, believing it was 'summat not for someone like me.' It may be considered that the 'universal adopted strategy for effectively denouncing the temptation to demean oneself is to naturalize difference, to turn it into second nature through inculcations and incorporation in the form of habitus' (Bourdieu 1994:122).

So what changed? On reading other learners' poetry she seemed totally amazed that people who lived on the same streets as her had penned such 'magic' . . . She voiced hope that 'if they can do it, who are just like me, then, so can I'. Her position in the 'field' changed. A common metaphor Bourdieu (1994) uses to represent the field is games. At first glance, a seemingly innocent metaphor, but on deeper probing it reveals how these fields (for example education) are sites controlled by the dominant class. A means to win advantage – but not always fairly – and in doing so pass on their capital (for example linguistic capital) to the next generation and if left un-tackled the ball rolls to the next and next.

Carol challenged her position in the 'field', grabbed the ball and ran with it. She soaked up the lessons, even asking for more poetry. Words began to really inspire her and rather than running from words she began to embrace language as something she had the right to use. She described how on shaping sentences it really helped her to 'deal with those lousy feelings' that had crammed her life for too often like 'doubt failure and fear'.

Discovering she had flair in writing poetry helped her realise 'I used to think everyone was better, now I know we're all the same – equal like.' Taking control of language, she has kicked out a space in the field where her expectations, creativity and confidence no longer sit on the side-line. Each word is a winning goal, each poem a winning match. Carol wrote that:

> When I started a part-time course at college to improve my English – never in my wildest dreams did I think I would end up writing poetry. What got me thinking that just maybe I could was reading a poem that a girl called Linda had wrote about the race riots. As I read those powerful words how I wished I had her gift.
>
> When I was asked to have a go at writing a short poem myself – my heart jumped – yeah I wanted to, but to be honest I got stressed out, had sleepless nights. I felt out of my league. When I discussed this with Vicky, my tutor, she reassured me saying 'words are for everyone' and slowly taking small steps then bigger and bigger I grew braver – words I never thought I'd use sprang in my head and onto the page. In fact once I wrote my first one, me Carol, who you might walk past in the street without a second glance, had words on a page that would stop your stride, I felt full of pride about that.

After that it just got so much easier and when I am feeling stressed and angry about something I find it good therapy to put my thoughts and feelings on paper in the form of a poem. One instance that springs to mind is one Friday night the other week when my granddaughter who's fifteen started playing me up yet again. Not listening to a word I say she stays out with her friends when she should be in for ten. I don't approve of her drinking – but she does – knocking drinks back she becomes abusive with me and shouts that I am always in her face. Upset, I went upstairs to calm down and write my feelings on my pad of paper I always carry with me. This helped me feel calmer. If I didn't have this means of expressing myself I don't know what I'd do – probably I'd just walk out of the house and round the streets, lost and angry as I've done so many times before. It's taken me until I'm sixty to find this way of dealing with life and the pain it sometimes throws at me – and yeah sometimes I wish I would have had this outlet when I was younger and life hit hard. But what matters is I've proved life gets better with age if you have the tool to help you find your way – for me the tools are the words in my poetry.

The creativity opened a space for transformation. This transformation saw a shift in Carol's habitus. Bourdieu positions the habitus as a socially constituted system of cognitive and motivating structures which produce and organise practices and their representations for the social agents. The lessons offered a critical space for Carol (and the other learners) to explore their creativity and their literacy practices. The hierarchy of taste and style which are embedded in culture are useful when considering Carol's attitude towards creativity. Poetry and art were classed for 'people not like us'. Bourdieu (1984) suggested the ways in which apparently distinctive and individualised consumption and leisure practices tend to betray their class origins. In order to challenge this hegemony of distinction which serves to oppress the working classes, judgment of taste must hold open a future that goes beyond the culture of the dominant or dominated. Figure 3.4 illustrates how the cycle of deprivation of capitals across the domains of education and family can be transformed though education and creative expression. This can lead to empowerment, ownership of language and creative expression, a rich habitus and the empowerment of communities.

This move towards embedding creativity into the curriculum is often difficult as college curricula (and school) often do not acknowledge the creativity that learners bring into the classroom. Their creativity is often masked in a process of symbolic violence where their hopes, desires and practices outside the class are not explored and instead, a dominant competency based model of literacy is delivered. Using multimodal approaches which includes poetry and images, can be a move towards reflection and transformation, leading to a shift to the habitus systems of dispositions that generate behaviours, including perceptions, expectations, beliefs and actions in a particular context. In this case creativity can arise

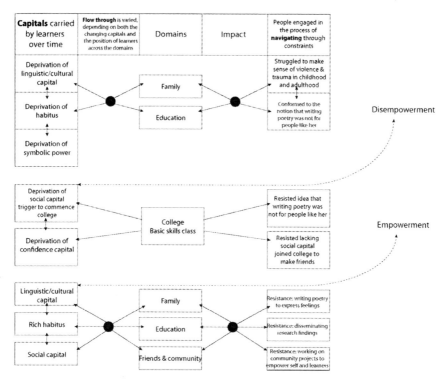

*Figure 3.4* Cycle of deprivation of capitals, transformation though education and creative expression, empowerment and ownership of language

from sharing creativity and encouraging learners to think beyond a competence based approach to literacy. The confidence that arises from creativity can also empower the learners in other fields of their private and public life.

## Curriculum design and working with learners

The PAR led to the negotiation of the structure and content of the curriculum and was a key part of my drive as a research practitioner. There was an emphasis on facilitating the learners to view themselves as sharing power with myself where they felt confident enough to express themselves. A key drive of the curriculum design was to recognise the socially situated literacies the learners brought to the classroom. The PAR facilitated this, allowing us to explore our lives in the public as well as private domains. Moving from a deficit model, this legitimised the experiences and knowledge of the learners across the domains of their life.

The shift in the power position in relation to my role as teacher and researcher allowed the learners to be co-investigators in the research and, from our findings, co-constructors of the curriculum. The pedagogy allowed critical discussions where we were able to unpick the themes of the research and see how this could be further expanded on and illuminated in the lesson. One theme that came up was having the space to plan for the future and looking at the steps needed to be taken to move forward. This lead to developing activities which valued the learners' everyday practices within the classroom (e.g. Barton and Hamilton 1998; Barton et al. 2006; Johnson et al. 2010). We looked at different people's experiences and learning from each other, identified different steps which could be used to reach our goals.

This allowed us to reflect on barriers and how we could address them to move forward. The sharing of the barriers provided the opportunity to critically discuss the violence and trauma the learners had experienced in their lives. Issues related to addressing violence and trauma were then embedded into the lesson and are now part of a set of national resources. The resources are also embedded into the teacher education programme, offering trainee teachers examples of more critical approaches to curriculum design which include opening up opportunities to address issues of violence which permeate through many learners' lives. Stories, poetry and images were used as foils to represent the generative themes in the lives of the learners (Duckworth 2008; Johnson et al. 2010; McNamara 2007).

## Discussion

The research created a critical space where the experience of the participants who do not fit with dominant ideologies (the school's invisible curriculum and New Labour's and the coalition government's individualism) are given voice and validated leading to the development of more meaningful knowledge. Subsequently, this knowledge aims to expand on and create concepts that are generated from the lived experience of the group rather than thrust upon it, resulting in explanatory power in the public and private domains of their lives. As identified by Thomas et al. (2012), learners' diverse backgrounds and experiences can have an impact on their learning. Teachers can use diversity positively to enhance the learning experience of individuals and the group, rather than seeking to normalise and elide difference. Indeed, many learners who attend adult literacy classes have often had to overcome significant barriers, including symbolic and physical violence,  to gain the confidence and courage to return to learning, in some cases bringing with them 'fear of violence, threat and intimidation' (see Barton et al. 2007:165). Offering a space both in the classroom and the community for the learners to share their narratives, for example, Carol's poetry, allowed the sharing of obstacles and solutions to overcome them. In this capacity the narratives are themselves a capital which can be pulled on by others to inspire and offer strategies to move forward. And Joanne's narrative offered an inspirational narrative related to her learning journey and overcoming obstacles, such as being poor, being in an abusive relationship and the power of education to transform her and her children's lives for the better. The learners were able to be actively involved in decision making and dialogue with the positive outcome of a democratic environment and culture being co-constructed both inside and outside the classroom. For many of the learners this inclusive approach to education and community action was the antithesis to what they had experienced previously. The research group facilitated the power of the collective over individual approaches. These bonds helped the learners to overcome the violence and trauma of school experiences where they were judged by the dominant culture for being poor and not being successful within the educational system. Indeed, even when learners have been in vulnerable situations, facing domestic violence or other social or emotional difficulties, adult literacy education can often be a critical space to support and empower them to take agency, no matter what their trajectory so far.

## Conclusion

The potential for resistance and counter hegemonic practice remains a challenge to teachers. Teachers need to be aware of how their beliefs and practices may be inclined by perceptions of learners' ability tied to class, gender and ethnicity and to challenge the reproductive tendencies these perceptions involve. As identified by Levy et al.:

> Literacy does not mean the same thing to everyone and varies across contexts. It is important to consider literacy in relation to access, attainment and social mobility, in terms of 'types' of literacy experiences, and in terms of individual, societal and political conceptions of literacy in the formation of social advantage and disadvantage.
>
> (2014:20–21)

The PAR allowed me to address the conflict for basic skills tutors between enacting the dominant ideologies of individualism and exploring the structural inequalities which have impacted on the learners' lives. It led to the negotiation of the structure and content of the CCCM curriculum and thus a model of teaching that embraced caring between the teacher and learner. Such emancipatory practices encourage autonomy and critical thinking, opening up spaces where learners and communities can ask questions, analyse and subsequently work through effective and meaningful strategies to enhance their situation, plan for their future and be active members of their communities (Duckworth 2014).

Indeed, in an educational environment where learners were valued and their socially situated literacies acknowledged and used, they were able to challenge the cycle of domination and symbolic violence; re-claiming spoilt identities of failure and transformed them to ones of success and empowerment.

## Notes

1  I employ Antonio Gramsci (1891–1937), a leading Marxist thinker, who used the term hegemony to signify the power of one social class over others, for example, the bourgeois hegemony. It embodies not only political and economic control, but also the ability of the dominant class to assign its own way of viewing the world so that those who are subordinated by it accept it as 'natural'. Gramsci's ideas have influenced popular education practices which I draw on, which include the adult literacy and consciousness-raising methods of Paulo Freire in his *Pedagogy of the Oppressed* (1996) and methods of participatory action research (PAR).
2  Human capital may be viewed from a micro-perspective, for example, the way the accumulation of knowledge and skills, such as literacy practices enables learners to increase their productivity and their earnings and macro, how this impacts on the productivity and wealth of the communities and societies they live. The dominant model of institutional literacies derives human capital from economic returns, such as employability.

## References

Archer, L., Hutchings, M. and Ross, A. (2003) *Higher Education and Social Class: Issues of exclusion and inclusion*. London: Routledge Falmer.

Barton, D. (1994) *Literacy: An Introduction to the Ecology of Written Language*. Oxford: Blackwell.

Barton, D. (2007). *Literacy: An introduction to the ecology of written language*. 2nd edn. Oxford: Blackwell.

Barton, D. and Hamilton, M. (1998) *Local Literacies: Reading and writing in one community*. London: Routledge.

Barton, D., Hamilton, M. and Ivanič, R. (eds) (2000) *Situated Literacies: Reading and writing in context*. Routledge: London and New York.

Barton, D., Ivanič, R., Appleby, Y., Hodge, R. and Tusting, K. (2006) *Relating Adults' Lives and Learning: Participation and engagement in different settings*. London: NRDC.

Barton, D., Ivanič, R., Appleby, Y., Hodge, R. and Tusting, K. (2004) *Adult Learners' Lives Project: Setting the scene, progress report*. Lancaster: NRDC, Lancaster University.

Barton, D., Ivanič, R., Appleby, Y., Hodge, R. and Tusting, K. (2007) *Literacy, Lives and Learning*. London: Routledge.

Bernstein, B. (1971a) *Class, Codes and Control: Theoretical studies towards a sociology of language*, Vol. I. London: Routledge and Kegan Paul.

Bernstein, B (1971b) 'On the classification and framing of educational knowledge', in Young, M. F. D. (ed.) *Knowledge and Control: New directions for the sociology of education*. London: Collier-Macmillan, pp. 19–46.

Bourdieu, P. (1984) *Distinction: A social critique of the judgement of taste* (R. Nice, trans.). Cambridge, MA: Harvard University Press.

Bourdieu, P. (1991) *Language and Symbolic Power*. Cambridge, MA: Harvard University Press.

Bourdieu, P. (1994) *Language and Symbolic Power*. Cambridge: Polity Press.

Bourdieu, P. (2001) 'The forms of capital', in Granovetter, M. and Swedberg, R. (eds) *The Sociology of Economic Life*. Cambridge, MA: Westview Press, pp. 96–111.

Burke, P. J. (2006) '"Fair access?" Exploring gender, access and participation beyond entry to higher education', in Leathwood, C. and Francis, B. (eds) *Gender and Lifelong Learning: Critical feminist engagements*. London: Routledge, pp. 40–53.

Crowther, J., Hamilton, M. and Tett, L. (2006) *Powerful Literacies*. Leicester: NIACE.

Department for Education and Employment (DfEE) (1999) *A Fresh Start: The report of a working group chaired by Sir Claus Moser*. London: Department for Education and Employment.

Department for Education and Employment (DfEE) (2001) 'Executive summary', *Skills for Life: The national strategy to improve adult literacy and numeracy skills*. Nottingham: DfEE Publications.

Department for Education and Skills (DfES) (2002) *Success for All*. London: DfES.

Duckworth, V. (2008) *Getting Better Worksheets: Adult literacy resources*. Warrington: Gatehouse Books.

Duckworth, V. (2010) 'Sustaining learning over time: it looks more like a Yellow Brick Road than a straightforward path for women experiencing violence', *Research and Practice in Adult Literacy*, 71: 19–20.

Duckworth, V. (2013) *Learning Trajectories, Violence and Empowerment amongst Adult Basic Skills Learners. Monograph: Educational Research*. London: Routledge.

Duckworth, V. (2014) Basic Skills Provision: a powerful tool for challenging inequality and empowering learners, their family and their local and wider communities. *Adults Learning* 25(40): 19–20.

Duckworth, V. and Brzeski, A. (Forthcoming) 'Literacy, learning and identity challenging the neo-liberal agenda through literacies, everyday practices and empowerment'. *Research in Post-compulsory Education in Training*.

Duckworth, V. and Cochrane, M. (2012) 'Spoilt for choice, spoilt by choice: Long-term consequences of limitations imposed by social background', *Journal of Education and Training*, 54(7): 579–591.

Duckworth, V. and Taylor, K. (2008) 'Words are for everyone', *Research and Practice in Adult Literacy*, 64: 30–328.

Duckworth, V. and Tummons, J. (2014) 'Neo-liberalism and social justice in post-compulsory education and training'. *Education and Training*, 56(7): 586–587.

Feeley, M. (2007) Adult Literacy and Affective Equality: Recognising the pivotal role of care in the learning relationship. Dublin University, unpublished PhD thesis.

Feeley, M. (2014) *Learning Care Lessons: Literacy, Love, Care and Solidarity*. London: Tufnell Press.

Field, J. (2000) *Lifelong Learning and the New Educational Order*. Stoke-on-Trent: Trentham Books.

Freire, P. (1996) *Pedagogy of the Oppressed*. London: Penguin.

Gee, J.P. (1996), *Social Linguistics and Literacies: Ideology in discourses*, 2nd edition. London: Routledge Falmer.

Gee, J.P. (2004) *Situated Language and Learning: A critique of traditional schooling*. London: Routledge.

Giroux, H. (1997) *Pedagogy and the Politics of Hope: Theory, culture, and schooling*. Boulder, CO: Westview Press.

Hamilton, M. (1996) 'Literacy and adult basic education,' in Fieldhouse, R. (ed.), *A History of Modern British Adult Education*. Leicester: NIACE.

Hamilton, M. (2012) *Literacy and the Politics of Representation*. Abingdon, UK: Routledge.

Hamilton, M. and Hillier, Y. (2006) *Changing Faces of Adult Literacy, Language and Numeracy: A critical history*. Stoke on Trent, UK and Sterling, USA: Trentham Books.

Heath, S. B. (1983) *Ways with Words: Language, life and work in communities and classrooms*. Cambridge: Cambridge University Press.

Johnson, C., Duckworth, V., McNamara, M. and Apelbaum, C. (2010) 'A tale of two adult learners: from adult basic education to degree completion', *National Association for Developmental Education Digest*, 5(1): 57–67.

Labov, W. (1972) *Language in the Inner City: Studies in the Black English Vernacular*. Philadelphia: University of Pennsylvania Press.

Lankshear, C. and McLaren, P. (eds) (1992), *Critical Literacy: Politics, praxis, and the postmodern*. Albany, NY: State University of New York Press.

Lankshear, C. (1993) 'Functional literacy from a Freirean point of view', in McLaren, P. and Leonard, P. (eds), *Paulo Freire: A critical encounter*. New York: Routledge, pp. 90–118.

Leathwood, C. (2006) 'Gendered constructions of lifelong learning and the learner in the UK policy context', in Leathwood, C. and Francis, B. (eds) *Gender and Lifelong Learning: Critical feminist engagements*. London: Routledge, pp. 40–53.

Levy, R., Little, S., Clough, P., Nutbrown, C., Bishop, J., Lamb, T., and Yamada-Rice, D. (2014) *Attitudes to Reading and Writing and their Links with Social Mobility 1914–2014: An evidence review*. Sheffield: Booktrust.

Luttrell, W. (1997) *School-smart and Mother-wise: Working-class women's identity and schooling*. New York: Routledge.

Lynch, K., Lyons, M. and Barry, U. (eds) (2008) *The Gendered Order of Caring: Women in contemporary Ireland*. Dublin: New Ireland Press.

Macedo, D. (1994) *Literacies of Power: What Americans are not allowed to know*. Boulder, CO: Westview Press.

McNamara, M. (2007) *Getting Better*. Warrington: Gatehouse Books.

Morrish, E., Horsman, J. and Hofer, J. (2002) *Take on the Challenge: A Sourcebook from the Women, Violence, and Adult Education Project*. Washington, DC: United States Department of Education, Women's Educational Equity (WEEA) Program.

O'Brien, M. (2005) 'Mothers as educational workers: Mothers' emotional work at their children's transfer to second-level schooling', *Irish Educational Studies* 24(2–3): 223–243.

Papen, U. (2005) *Adult Literacy as Social Practices: More than skills*. London: Routledge.

Papen, U. (2007) *Literacy and Globalisation: Reading and writing in times of social and cultural change*. London: Routledge.

Puwar, N. (2004) *Space Invaders: Race, gender and bodies out of place*. Oxford: Berg.

Reay, D. (2000) 'A useful extension of Bourdieu's conceptual framework? Emotional capital as a way of understanding mothers' involvement in their children's education', *Sociological Review*, 48: 568–585.

Reay, D. (2005) 'Beyond consciousness? The psychic landscape of class.' *Sociology*, 395: 911–928.

Shor, I. (1992) *Empowering Education: Critical Teaching for Social Change*. Chicago, IL: University of Chicago Press.

Shor, I. (1993) 'Education is politics: Paulo Freire's critical pedagogy', in McLaren, P. and Leonard, P. (eds) *Paulo Freire: A critical encounter*. London: Routledge, pp. 25–35.

Steedman, C. (1988) '"The mother made conscious": the historical development of primary school pedagogy', in Woodhead, M. and McGrath, A. (eds) *Family, School and Society*. Buckingham: The Open University, pp. 82–95.

Street, B. (1984), *Literacy in Theory and Practice*. Cambridge: Cambridge University Press.

Thomas, L., Bland, D. C. and Duckworth, V. (2012) 'Teachers as advocates for widening participation and Lifelong Learning', *Journal of Widening Participation and Education* 14(2): 40–58.

# Chapter 4

# Survey literacies

*Mary Hamilton*

## Introduction

### Setting the scene: how literacy is changing and what I mean by "survey literacies"

There are many ways in which the landscapes of literacy are changing in the twenty-first century. These include changes in technological and other ways of communicating as well as the political and cultural revaluing of forms of the written word. Many of these changes are creative and productive, some are eagerly claimed or resisted, some are open-access and social. From social networking sites, blogs and fan-fiction to online educational courses and the mixing of cultural genres, the potential of literacy has never been greater but so are the risks and challenges its poses in its new forms. This chapter is about a particular set of powerful literacies that are proving immensely productive but also have social effects that are potentially negative or risky. I am calling these "survey literacies" and there are three parts to my discussion. First, I will present the disciplines of production of large scale testing and assessment of literacy as one aspect of the use of "big data" and statistics. Second, I will explore the literacies of test-taking and scoring behaviors and third, the practices involved in interpreting, displaying and applying the results of surveys within policy and practice. Following the approach of the New Literacy Studies which informs this book (Barton, 2007; Brandt, 2009 and Street and Lefstein, 2007) and socio-material theory (Fenwick et al., 2011); I will elaborate the activities, history and social relations involved in each of these sets of literacy practices and draw some conclusions about their significance to the field as evolving forms and what they tell us about the role of literacy in contemporary social ordering.

International surveys of literacy have become increasingly important over the last 20 years, organized by a range of agencies including the Organization for Economic Co-operation and Development (OECD, 2000, 2013), UNESCO (UNESCO, 2009) and the European Union (Dale and Robertson, 2009). National governments commit considerable funding to these surveys and countries then compare themselves against one another other using the results. Curricula, performance indicators and assessments are shaped by these measures.

In this process, our views of what counts as literacy, its goals and who literacy learners are is also formed. Standardized profiles of achievement are highly valued, while at the same time perceived by many to be at odds with the everyday literacy practices of both teachers and their students. This chapter describes some of the background to these tests, how they are constructed and the rationales used for them. Indeed, as I write this chapter, the last six months have seen the release of the first results from the survey of adult skills (the Programme for the International Assessment of Adult Competencies or PIAAC). In addition, the latest round of PISA results have also been released, measuring the literacy, numeracy and scientific skills of 15-year-old populations. In making my argument I will refer to both of these survey events, especially the findings of the PIAAC and how these were created and interpreted to public audiences.

Drawing on the above, I will argue that the numerical results of such surveys are far from neutral "facts," rather they are inevitably constructed and interpreted in particular ways through the processes of translating literacy into numbers. They also serve wider global agendas that are important for researchers, practitioners and literacy advocates to engage with. I explore what these surveys can tell us about literacy and how they tell us, how they affect the ways we visualise what literacy is, who needs it and why. These issues will be linked into the bigger landscape of educational policy and also emerging trends in the use of "big data" by commerce and government to make evidence-informed decisions and to monitor practice.

I will argue that with such enthusiasms now driving many educational and research initiatives, critical debate is needed about how the "facts" about literacy are constructed and how they reach into our everyday lives and imaginations. Such debate can only rest on a good understanding of how and why these tests have been constructed, what is involved in taking the tests, and in scoring and interpreting them. These understandings amount to "survey literacies" – how reading and writing are being measured and the social relations within which this is being done. We are all involved in survey literacies, whether we choose to be or not – some helping to produce the tests, some as test-takers or mentors of those preparing for the tests, or many of us as consumers of the media reports about the tests that circulate widely. Sometimes we take up these results ourselves to advocate for literacy education or to develop research and in this case we become part of the process of dispersing them through the public imagination.

There is a bigger context within which the development of the international surveys of literacy should be understood. These surveys are designed to contribute to policy decisions as part of a more general trend toward "governance by data" which has been pointed out by many researchers interested in how decision-making about social policy is changing (see Meyer and Benavot, 2013; Ozga et al., 2011). These changes are, in part, political in nature, fuelled by the values of neoliberalism which sees education, including basic education and literacy, as a product that can be bought, sold and packaged within a global marketplace (see Rizvi and Lingard, 2010). Evidenced-based policy is sought to ensure that the most productive use is made of public funds and data is needed to inform such policy and to determine "what works" (Pawson, 2002). The search for universal and global solutions to policy problems that can be exchanged across national contexts, leads us to find ways of measuring performance that will enable comparison and ranking with others. In turn this leads to standard-ization and the elision of national and cultural differences. These measures are claimed to be rational, precise and universal (Steiner-Khamsi, 2003). This desire is reinforced by the possibilities offered by digital technologies to generate huge amount of data that can be used to monitor performance and to feedback to third parties information about the behavior and preferences of individuals. The effects of these moves are to increase public reporting frameworks with all the associated issues of privacy, ethics and surveillance.

Ian Hacking (1990) has written about the historical precedents for this enthu-siasm for data and he documents the "avalanche of numbers" that enthused social engineers at the end of the nineteenth century in Europe and the US. The science of statistics means "numbers in the service of the state" and politics and statistics have always been closely connected (Porter, 1996). This enthusiasm for numbers has always been double edged. Good data is a fundamental support to the administration and politics of liberal democracy yet it also offers unprec-edented powers to control and define – as in colonial administrations (Mitchell, 2002). Rose refers to the optimistic expectation of the liberal state that num-bers can replace old relations of status, rank with objectivity and truth. But he also points out the implicit loss of trust involved in relying on objective mea-surement and how citizens become complicit in measuring themselves against others – developing what he terms "the calculating self" (Rose, 1998).

There has been much interest of late in "big data" and the role it can play in decision making in diverse areas of areas of social activity (business, entertain-ment, science, government, advertising, healthcare, to name a few). Journalist James Glanz refers to big data as the amount of information "sloshing through the public network that spans the planet" and the technologies for extract-ing this data and subjecting it to computer analysis (Glanz, NYT August 17 2013). By employing a combination of modern artificial intelligence, machine learning and statistical techniques, extremely large and complex data sets can be "mined" in a variety of ways to reveal relationships, patterns and insights not easily discoverable through standard database management tools and data processing applications.

In turn, this capacity for capturing and mining data has fuelled the fast pro-gressing field of learning analytics generated from the data traces left by online interactions between learners, teachers and administrators. Long and Siemens 2011 explain:

> Listening to a classroom lecture or reading a book leaves limited trails. A hallway conversation essentially vaporizes as soon as it is concluded.

However, every click, every Tweet or Facebook status update, every social interaction, and every page read online can leave a digital footprint. Additionally, online learning, digital student records, student cards, sensors, and mobile devices now capture rich data trails and activity streams. These learner-produced data trails provide valuable insight into what is actually happening in the learning process and suggest ways in which educators can make improvements.

(Siemens and Long, 2011)

This knowledge can be employed for a variety of purposes, among which are to allow learners to reflect on their activity and progress in relation to that of others as well as to assist teachers and support staff in predicting, identifying and supporting learners who may require additional attention and intervention (MacNeill and Powell, 2012). The use of big data in the educational sphere has potentially revolutionary applications, for example in the development of MOOCS (Massive Open Online Courses).

From this discussion we can see why we need to be concerned with survey literacies and why and how they are proliferating. They tie in with global agendas of neo-liberalism and pose questions of agency and power: who is collecting data, on whom and for what purposes? The expensive developments of survey literacies as part of the enthusiasm for big data take place in a particular economic context where neo-liberal ideals predominate. Quantified data – whether through international tests or the data captured from learning systems – promises more effective educational policy and pedagogies. It also carries the risks of excessive surveillance and the standardization and narrowing of what counts as literacy since what is measurable becomes visible and most valued. The result, according to some commentators, is that public education is being lifted out of its local cultural context and its very meaning "is being recast from a project aimed at forming national citizens and nurturing social solidarity to a project driven by economic demands and labor market orientations" (Meyer and Benavot, 2013:10).

In the following sections I will explore how the international surveys are constructed and how publics are imagined, constructed and enrolled into their measurement projects.

## The literacies of test-making: producing large scale international surveys and tests

This section discusses how facts about literacy are currently being constructed through increasingly sophisticated technologies of numerical measurement. These are deployed through international surveys that compare performance across different countries and cultures and encourage us to imagine "literacy" as a quantified thing that can be calculated, embedded in and related to other measured social goods. Numbers are increasingly mobilized to make a persuasive impact in the mass media and the public imagination.

The Organization for Economic Cooperation and Development (OECD), UNESCO and the European Union, along with many national governments, have for some years now invested heavily to produce internationally comparable statistics on literacy competencies. The best known of these is the OECD's Programme for International Student Assessment (PISA), which is extensively reported in the media and used as a basis for educational policy decisions (see, for example, the recent move in the UK to bench-mark GCSE exam results to Chinese performance on the PISA test).[1] The latest development in international testing is the Programme for the International Assessment of Adult Competencies (PIAAC), also known as the Adult Skills Survey (OECD, 2013). The PIAAC has so far been conducted in 23 countries. A second round will take place in 2012–2016 in another nine countries, whilst the OECD is calling for more countries, including low- and middle-income countries, to join. PIAAC builds on both PISA and the International Adult Literacy Survey (IALS) and is the result of the combined efforts of the OECD and the European Union. In a related development, UNESCO's Literacy Assessment and Monitoring Programme (UNESCO, 2009) aims to provide the diagnostic information required to monitor and improve literacy skills worldwide and to inform national policies.

The aim of these surveys is to assess the literacy achievements of populations for employability and for citizenship within complex environments of cultural diversity, changing knowledge requirements and technologies. They are based on an information processing view of reading and writing and the test items are carefully constructed to mimic real-life texts that will be recognizable across national contexts. However, these items are then used in a decontextualized way which encourages those being tested to discard their local knowledge and to look for meaning and answers only in the texts themselves. As we will see later, this model of literacy, can be problematic when it is put into practice, since it signals a confusing version of "reality" that is picked up in different ways by people taking the test.

Categories created through numbers are not only descriptive but normalizing devices. That is, they define not just what *is*, but what should be. Determining what or who counts as eligible to be a citizen or a literate person also shapes the flip side – non-citizens, and illiterates who are stigmatized as deviant outsiders. Their characteristics and experiences are devalued by the classification system and therefore discounted. Furthermore, the collectivities defined through measuring are not self-constituted social groups, but statistical artefacts. People frequently do not identify themselves as a member of the category they have been allocated to or excluded from and that is why so much effort needs to go into publicity campaigns to get people to recognize themselves in the appropriate way.

Once the categories have been identified and accepted into research and popular discourse, they become solid "facts" that we rarely question. This can most strikingly be demonstrated by looking historically at categories that once did not exist, but are now fundamental to our understanding of social reality. For example, the social class categories that are now used in every survey were invented at the end of the nineteenth century by Charles Booth (see Hamilton, 2012: 27) and we treat them as facts although they were generated from a particular time, place and set of cultural and economic circumstances.

Numbers are essential to developing and applying these processes of categorization. They are central to systems of auditing, counting and measuring peoples' achievements and the outcomes related to their performance through statistics and surveys (see Power, 1999 and Strathern, 2000). The translation of the arbitrary and fuzzy categories that numbers rest on, into hard and accepted facts, and the appearance of accuracy that they present, are their most powerful assets for policy and research. Such "black boxed" categories achieve scientific credibility and become rationales for action, aided by the fact that many people do not feel in control of numbers and therefore do not approach them critically.

They are useful to politicians and civil servants who are pushed to justify their expenditure on policies: how much, more, or less, to what effect. Since numbers facilitate comparisons across incomparable spaces of time and place they are also useful to current processes of internationalization, enabling qualifications indicators of social well-being and quality to be harmonized across global market places. International networks and new technologies make such counting and comparison easier, faster and more flexible.

The international tests involve a complex sequence of transformations between everyday literacy practices and measured numerical scores. Radhika Gorur (2011) conducted interviews with those involved in creating the PISA test and has traced the different stages at which the methodology progressively constrains and shapes the facts that are produced at the end of this process. The decisions made at each point involve difficult negotiations between countries that have different values and debates in relation to their education systems. These decisions include:

- choice of items to represent domains of knowledge as well as the conceptual framework behind these choices;
- how to translate the items across cultures and languages in the search for equivalence;
- choice of comparative samples of people to test representative of the populations in each country;
- agreement on methods of data collection under the different circumstances of each country;
- agreement on statistical techniques to be used; and
- interpretation of the indicators that are produced.

## The literacies of test-taking and scoring behaviors

When we think about the literacies that are taught in educational contexts, the reading and writing involved in taking tests is not seen to be central – or if it is, then it tends to be discussed as "teaching to the test" also known as the "washback" effect: a problematic distortion of the teaching and learning that is the main purpose of education. While I am in sympathy with this view of the distorting effects of testing, what interests me in this discussion is to analyze, from the literacy as social practice point of view, the social practices of test-taking literacies and to deal with them in a "symmetrical" way (Latour, 2012) – that is to accept that such practices are a part of contemporary education, embedded in different ways in it and are therefore not to be treated as an aberration, but as a specific landscape to be scrutinized and taken seriously.

If we are looking at test-taking in a local school environment, the behaviors may not look so different from other aspects of education, especially where whole-class and text-book or worksheet approaches to literacy are dominant so that students become used to "schooled knowledge" as a special kind that is different from everyday knowing (see Singh, 2002). Formal testing may take place in a special room, under specially controlled rules – silence; individual work without communicating with others; regulated use of technological aids such as calculators, mobile phones or reference books; using paper and pencil or a digital interface; specific timing; writing in a special test booklet and using other materials which are not released beforehand. There may be special conditions for people with disabilities. All of these controls specify particular and unusual material conditions and performances that are distinct from everyday literacy practices in other settings (see Lawn and Grosvenor, 2005; Nespor, 1997).

There are restrictions placed on the language used for the test and particular understanding of the format and demands of the test are needed. If it is multiple choice, you can only tick one answer, for example. If a more narrative answer is required, then criteria for scoring are more complex and it is important for the test-taker to be able to put themselves in the shoes of the scorer to decide what will count as a "good" response.

When we are interested in the testing of adult skills, sometimes the same schooled practices are in place also. But most often, the testing takes place in peoples' homes or workplaces, or perhaps a job center, more like the way that household surveys are conducted for the census. The conditions placed on reading and writing in these situations may be different as is the degree to which the process can be closely controlled. In the PIAAC for the first time, people were invited to enter their answers on the screen of a digital device brought into their homes by Tsatsaroni and Evans (2013) speculate about the possible effects of this new medium on people's performance on the test, depending on how familiar they are with digital technologies and interfaces and how far the task represented by the test-item would actually be encountered on-line in day-today settings. Evans suggests that the enforcement of such survey conditions and processes may reduce the ecological validity of the test which does not take account of generational and national differences in communication practices.

If we look even further from local educational contexts, people are being asked to take tests in many different countries around the world, in cities and in rural environments, in cultural circumstances that vary greatly and we have few descriptions of what survey literacies look like in these diverse places. One such description has been offered by Maddox (2013) who, as an anthropologist, has had the unusual opportunity to accompany test-administrators on their journeys into Mongolia. He describes the setting, the process and the local etiquette in the following quotation:

> The desert is sparsely populated and home to nomadic pastoralists who herd camels, horses, goats, sheep and cows. The assessments took place in people's homes (whether conventional houses in urban centres or in gers – the traditional, round, felt covered nomadic homes). Urban and nomadic homes are often one room constructions. That imposes certain dynamics on the testing situation. The Gobi desert is bitterly cold in November, so the testing team, the respondent and their family, including babies and young children, the local guide and driver, interpreter and the author were frequently present during assessment events. The adults would usually be offered tea and milk-based snacks while the assessment took place.
>
> (Maddox, 2014:4)

He explains how it was impossible in these circumstances to keep everyday life from intruding because the ideal of an individual test taker and tester working together under controlled conditions violates the assumptions of family relationships and status expectations: "respondents attempted to involve other people – the tester and family members to help them to complete the assessment task – asking for guidance, checking out the ground rules of the assessment" (Maddox, 2014:4).

While this might seem an extreme example of the mismatch between international tests and lived experience, the dynamics are recognizable to any researcher who has carried out data collection in homes or communities.

Maddox also points out how another familiar issue – that of motivation and persistence – has a great effect on test scores, since incomplete or untried items are scored as "incorrect". He goes on to present two different examples of test items that caused difficulties for the Mongolian test-takers. The difficulties centred around the central assumption of the test (mentioned earlier) that the answers to the test item can be found solely in the texts presented and that test-takers are required to put aside their local and contextual knowledge when taking the test.

On the one hand, an item about the Mongolian camel was very familiar to the nomadic people and their extensive contextual knowledge distracted them from the information in the text causing them to answer incorrectly. On the other hand, a test item based on an employment application form bore no relation at all to their experience of working in the desert and this interfered with their ability to make sense of the questions being asked. As a result, they tended to pass over this item rather than attempt to answer it. Both items had been crafted by the test-makers as "real life" materials, but in fact required the test-takers to bracket off their own contextual knowledge in a way that is the opposite of everyday literacy practice. The supposed "reality" of the textual world interfered with performance on the test: in one case the item was too real, and in the other it was not real enough.

## The literacies of interpreting, displaying and applying survey findings

When all the data has been assembled, it still has a long road to travel from the laptop on which it was collected, to the public audience and the policy forums for which it has been produced. Many transformations happen during this process, which mobilize the survey literacies of different groups of specialists and communicators. Once the data has been collected and scored by the interviewer/tester in the field, it is passed to another group of experts who put together the individual test results with others for that country and eventually pass these aggregated findings on to the international agencies where they are analyzed using computer-based statistical packages.

Not only is the data subjected to statistical techniques and tests which shape the results in particular ways, but the findings produced from these have then to be presented in reports, or websites using a whole array of visualizations and translated into the many languages of receiving countries. The international agencies coordinating the surveys (UNESCO, the OECD and the European Union) are active in these transformation processes and have extensive experience of crafting such reports and interpreting them to potential users.

The devices of layout, color, graphics, and tables are sophisticated and designed to be attractive and accessible (Tufte, 2006). The PIAAC website created by the OECD includes an interactive section, where someone from a particular country can call up the findings from their own context highlighted in relation to other countries and look at different distributions of adult skills according to age, employment status, gender and so on (http://www.oecd. org/site/piaac/country-specific-material.htm). Such websites actively draw the user into the survey findings and invite them to make their own selections and interpretations to pass on to others, co-producing the findings for particular audiences.

The OECD produces its own summaries of the findings which are integrated into press releases. These are organized both by individual country and with international comparisons that emphasize particular distributions and variables deemed to be significant. For example, in the PIAAC findings for the UK, an unusual pattern was identified whereby older adults scored more highly on literacy and numeracy than younger adults. The summaries and press releases repeated these figures in the national UK media. Initially they are presented as factual news, often with little elaboration or understanding of the surveys themselves. Comment, however, is quick to follow as the already selected figures are considered in relation to the league table of nations and interpreted again within current educational and social debates (see Steiner-Khamsi, 2003). The PIAAC figures highlighted for the UK, for example, were integrated into on-going debates about the quality of education, economic recession and unemployment rates of young people.

Contemporary media are quite complex, however, and in many countries they now include opportunities for members of the public to express their own views on the commentaries offered by media and academic experts via comments placed on online articles, through Twitter and other social media. An item from one of the main daily Spanish newspapers, El Mundo (El Mundo, October 2013) is an interesting example of this. Spain came bottom of the PIAAC league table and alongside the results, the newspaper reproduced some of the test items and invited readers to try them out. They also videoed "adults in the street" attempting to answer the questions and this video was available on the newspaper's online site. Nearly 400 comments were received from readers on the items representing the whole spectrum of views about the survey. There were many who expressed shock and disbelief of the findings and some who acknowledged them and raised issues of educational reform and politics by way of explanation. The great majority of comments leapt into a detailed discussion of the content of the items, the difficulties and ambiguities of translating them and the possible political agendas behind the setting of such a test. There was little knowledge of the actual origins of the test and how it had been conducted, although a few people queried the sample and who had chosen the items. One commentator suggested that there was a good deal of national hurt pride in evidence in the discussion and many of the comments made strong links with much broader political, religious and cultural debates.

We can see from this that once the data has been assembled there are still many steps of interpretation that take place as the survey findings are incorporated into public and specialist debates. It is possible to challenge the interpretation of the results in different ways – for example to question the validity of the tests themselves, or the interpretation or "spin" put on them by expert commentators. Discussions about technical validity, however, tend to occur rather far down the chain of communications and rarely surface in the headline news. The Spanish example may be a rare one of these that is made possible only by making available the actual content of the test to the members of the public subjected to it.

Rarely questioned either in the media coverage is what the historian Harvey Graff (1979) has identified as the "the literacy myth" – a belief in literacy as an independent variable which is "a necessary precursor to and invariably results in economic development, democratic practice, cognitive enhancement, and upward social mobility." Current international surveys act to reinforce this myth with its burden of expectation and promise for literacy that is not upheld by the historical evidence. One key aspect of survey literacies is to be able to critically engage with the assumptions on which the apparently scientific evidence from the international tests is based. I will go on to discuss the importance of this more fully in the final section.

## Critical understanding: survey literacies through the lens of the NLS

If we see literacy as part of social practice, as the contributors to this volume do, then we need to explore all the varieties and discourses of literacy situated in the many contexts of everyday life. Meanings of literacy are situated and a matter of discourse rather than essential definition. Many definitions can and do co-exist, therefore, and each tells an interesting story about the social relations, discourses and agencies that lie behind them and the vision of literacy that these promote. In Hamilton (2012) I present a variety of historical examples of different visions for literacy, ranging from the moral crusades of the educational pioneer Hannah More in eighteenth-century Britain, to the liberation literacies of the Nicaraguan campaign in the 1970s.

The current international surveys of literacy are working towards the vision of finding one authoritative definition for literacy worldwide. I have argued in this chapter that this is both misguided and dangerous and ultimately dysfunctional for policy since the single definition leads to inappropriate policy responses that ignore local realities and practices. We need therefore to be aware of the new ways of imagining literacy that are brought into being through the international surveys and how these tie in strongly with the global agendas and logic of neo-liberalism. We need to equip ourselves with the "survey literacies" necessary to critique them. From a set of numerical associations a causal argument is constructed about the simple effects of literacy skills on economic development and prosperity, individual and collective. This locates the cause of economic difficulty and inequality in the skills deficits of individuals and shifts the responsibility for these ills onto the most disadvantaged and vulnerable groups in the population. Reflecting on the attractions of this analysis Graff says:

> The power of the literacy myth lies in the first place in its resiliency, durability, and persistence. It serves to organize, simultaneously focus but obscure, and offer an explanation for an impressive array of social, economic, and political assumptions, expectations, observations, and theories, on the one hand, and institutions, policies, and their workings, on the other hand. Powerful contradictions lie at its core and in its consequences. As noted, socio-cultural myths, like the literacy myth, are never wholly false. Otherwise they would not gain acceptance or hegemony.
>
> (Graff, 2010)

Limited access to literacy is indeed associated with poverty and inequality and that is why many of us advocate for it. To claim it is a central and single cause of these demographic patterns is, however, a misuse of big data and a distortion of our imagination of literacy. Thus, the data generated from the surveys is organizing our knowledge of adult literacy and our responses to it. Policy analysts are under pressure to align their analysis of local problems with already existing global solutions – that is, the global solution frames the problem and is "borrowed" to address it. As Gita Steiner-Khamsi (2013) says, we need to question these solutions and the evidence that underlies them to dismantle what she called the three fallacies of the "what went right" analysis: rationality, precision and universality.

The final "survey literacy" we need then, is a critical appreciation of the purposes and effects of the international tests and there are several good reasons to be sceptical of their promises. First, there are issues of who has agency and power within the testing regimes: who is collecting data on whom? Meyer and Benavot (2013:12) list the powerful effects of international testing organisations on national policy and practice as they define new tasks to be carried out; create new social actors and motivations for them to act on and transfer not simply policy solutions, but new models of political organisation and governance around the world. These agencies claim superior expert knowledge but are still situated in local centers of calculation with their own distinct purposes and limited perspectives.

Second, the survey industry is expensive. Its high credibility moves it to center stage and this crowds out other kinds of knowledge and research, submerging other voices in what should be debates about the nature and purposes of literacy and research into ways of constructing pedagogy and curriculum with adult learners. Tests designed as national benchmarks have a habit of slipping inappropriately into individual tests of suitability for entrance to jobs and educational screening and begin to shape curricula and pedagogies too (as described earlier for the UK, see also Pinsent-Johnson, forthcoming).

While we do not need to be mathematicians in order to challenge the facts of international tests, those engaging in literacy advocacy in the twenty-first century do need to understand something about how the tests are constructed, be able to read the seductive visual displays of data and keep informed about the politics behind them. Equally important is to argue for the necessity of local situated studies for understanding the nature of literacy on the ground. Advocates need to hold our ground with these understandings and to keep on asserting the diversity of experience and purposes for literacy, calling the generalizations to account (see Brown et al., 2014).

Finally, as Meyer and Benavot (2013) suggest, we also need to imagine alternative futures for international cooperation, in which collaboration, exchanging ideas and borrowing practice across borders and institutions results in diversification and innovation instead of standardization and narrowing of education:

> Comparative study can facilitate  rich cross-cultural learning in which long-standing cultural practices are honored and taken seriously, even as countries innovate and selectively adopt best practices as they learn from results of peers. Results would focus on specific comparisons of specific practices and findings, leading to reflection and probing: "instead of

travelling troupes of IQ test-makers and implementers, we would have groups of teachers and administrators visiting and perhaps interning in the school systems of their peers". (2013: 22)

To bring such a vision into being will require sustained engagement with current testing regimes and the survey literacies they entail.

## References

Barton, D. (2007). *Literacy: An introduction to the ecology of written language.* 2nd edn. Oxford: Blackwell.

Brandt, D. (2009). *Literacy and learning: Reflections on writing, reading, and society.* Hoboken, NJ: John Wiley & Sons.

Brown, T., Yasukawa, K. and Black, S. (2014). Seeing and hearing: examining production workers' literacy and numeracy practices in a context of crisis. *Studies in Continuing Education,* (ahead-of-print), 1–13.

Dale, R. and Robertson, S. (2009). *Globalisation and Europeanisation in education.* Oxford: Symposium Books.

El Mundo (2013) ¿Aprobaría usted el examen de la OCDE? Available online: http://www.elmundo.es/elmundo/2013/10/07/espana/1381181039.html#comentarios Last accessed 27 August 2014.

Evans, J. (2013). Results from PIAAC on the way: Reading reports from international surveys of adult skills [with Anna Tsatsaroni, Tine Wedege, Keiko Yasukawa] Paper presented at ALM-20, University of South Wales, 1–4 July 2013.

Fenwick, T., Edwards, R. and Sawchuk, P. (2011). *Emerging approaches to educational research: Tracing the socio-material.* Abingdon, UK: Routledge.

Glanz, J. (2013). Is big data an economic big dud? *New York Times,* August 17. Available online: http://mobile.nytimes.com/2013/08/18/sunday-review/is-big-data-an-economic-big-dud.html?from=sunday-review&_r=0 Last accessed 27 August 2014.

Gorur, R. (2011). ANT on the PISA trail: Following the statistical pursuit of certainty. *Educational Philosophy and Theory,* 43(s1): 76–93.

Gorur, R. (2014). Towards a sociology of measurement in education policy. *European Educational Research Journal,* 13(1): 58–72.

Graff, H. J. (1979). *The literacy myth: Literacy and social structure in the nineteenth-century city. Studies in social discontinuity.* New York: Academic Press.

Graff, H. J. (2010). The literacy myth at thirty. *Journal of Social History,* 43(3): 635–661.

Grek, S. (2010). International organisations and the shared construction of policy 'problems': Problematisation and change in education governance in Europe. *European Educational Research Journal,* 9(3): 396–406.

Hacking, I. (1990). *The taming of chance.* Cambridge: Cambridge University Press.

Hamilton, M. (2012). *Literacy and the politics of representation.* Abingdon, UK: Routledge.

Latour, B. (2012). *We have never been modern.* Cambridge, MA: Harvard University Press.

Lawn, M. and Grosvenor, I. (2005). *Materialities of schooling: Design, technology, objects, routines.* Oxford: Symposium Books.

MacNeill, S. and Powell, S. (2012). Institutional readiness for analytics. Centre for Interoperability Standards (CETIS) Analytics Series, 1(8). Available online: http://www-jime.open.ac.uk/jime/article/viewArticle/2014-07/html Last accessed 27 August 2014.

Maddox, B. (2013). Inside the assessment machine: The life and times of a test item paper presented at the Literacy as Number International Symposium, London June 17th.

Meyer, H.-D. and Benavot, A. (eds) (2013). *PISA, power, and policy: The emergence of global educational governance.* Oxford: Symposium Books.

Mitchell, T. (2002). *Rule of experts: Egypt, techno-politics, modernity.* Berkeley, CA: University of California Press.

Nespor, J. (1997). *Tangled up in school: Politics, space, bodies, and signs in the educational process.* Mahwah, NJ: Lawrence Erlbaum.

OECD (2000). *Literacy in the Information Age.* Paris: OECD Publishing.

OECD (2013). *OECD Skills outlook 2013: First results from the survey of adult skills,* Paris: OECD Publishing. (http://dx.doi.org/10.1787/978926420456-en).

Ozga, J., Dahler-Larsen, P., Segerholm, C. and Simola, H. (eds) (2011). *Fabricating quality in education: Data and governance in Europe.* Abingdon, UK: Routledge.

Pawson, R. (2002). Evidence-based policy: The promise of realist synthesis. *Evaluation*, 8(3): 340–358.

Pinsent-Johnson (forthcoming). 'How learning inequality is made to happen: Curricularizing an international literacy test and classifying adult literacy learners' in Hamilton, M., Maddox B. and Addey, C.(eds) *Literacy as numbers: Researching the politics and practices of international literacy assessment regimes.* Cambridge: Cambridge University Press.

Porter, T. M. (1996). *Trust in numbers: The pursuit of objectivity in science and public life.* Princeton, NJ: Princeton University Press.

Power, M. (1999). *The audit society: Rituals of verification.* Oxford: Oxford University Press.

Rizvi, F. and Lingard, B. (2010). *Globalizing education policy.* Abingdon, UK: Routledge.

Rose, N. (1998). *Inventing ourselves: Psychology, power, and personhood.* Cambridge: Cambridge University Press.

Siemens, G. and Long, P. (2011). Penetrating the fog: Analytics in learning and education. *Educause Review*, 46(5): 30–32.

Singh, P. (2002). Pedagogising knowledge: Bernstein's Theory of the Pedagogic Device. *British Journal of Sociology of Education*, 23(4): 571–582.

Steiner-Khamsi, G. (2002). 'Reterritorializing educational import: Explorations into the politics of educational borrowing' in Nóvoa, A. and Lawn, M. (eds) *Fabricating Europe. The formation of an education space* (pp. 69–86). Dordrecht: Kluwer.

Steiner-Khamsi, G. (2003). The politics of league tables. *Online Journal of Social Science Education*, 2(1).

Steiner-Khamsi, G. (2013). 'What is wrong with the "what-went-right" approach in educational policy?' *European Educational Research Journal*, 12(1), 20–33.

Steiner-Khamsi, G. and Waldow, F. (eds) (2011). *Policy borrowing and lending in education.* Abingdon, UK: Routledge.

Strathern, M. (2000). *Audit cultures: Anthropological studies in accountability, ethics and the academy.* London: Routledge.

Street, B. and Lefstein, A. (2007). *Literacy: An advanced resource book for students.* Abingdon, UK: Routledge.

Tsatsaroni, A. and Evans, J. (2013). Adult numeracy and the totally pedagogised society: PIAAC and other international surveys in the context of global educational policy, *Educational Studies in Mathematics*, Special Issue on Social Theory in Mathematics Education (DOI: 10.1007/s10649-013-9470-x).

Tufte, E. R. (2006). *Beautiful evidence* (Vol. 1). Cheshire, CT: Graphics Press.

UNESCO Institute of Statistics (2009). *The next generation of literacy statistics: Implementing the literacy assessment and monitoring programme.* Montreal: UIS.

# Chapter 5

# Expanding the academic literacies frame

## Implications for understanding curriculum contexts in higher education

*Lynn Coleman and Mary R. Lea*

## Introduction

This chapter is concerned with higher education and the consequences of taking a social practice approach to literacy within curriculum contexts at university level. It raises questions about how a disciplinary or professional based curriculum implicitly privileges particular literacy practices and sets out to explore the processes by which these become embedded. The chapter begins by considering the contribution that work on academic literacies might make to thinking about a literacy curriculum in higher education. It elaborates this further through the exploration of a case study from a South African higher education context. This offers an analytic frame for understanding the relationship between how a curriculum is brought into being and the kinds of literacy practices that become valued. The chapter also indicates how practitioners in higher education might be able to facilitate curricula that are informed by ideas of textual practice and social and cultural approaches to literacy and learning.

Researchers who take a social and cultural approach to literacy in higher education generally locate their work in the field of academic literacies, a distinct area of study that began in the UK (Ivanič, 1998; Lea & Stierer, 2000; Lea & Street, 1998; Lillis, 2001). Its concern with academic writing as social practice emerged from its theoretical and methodological roots in applied linguistics, critical language studies and social anthropology. The use of the plural form, 'literacies', signals a conceptualization of literacy as a range of social and cultural practices around reading and writing in contexts. Initial research developed from a concern with understanding student writing. Researchers working across different contexts of higher education pointed to the significant gaps between students' and their lecturers' understanding of what was involved in writing at university. Researchers took a critical lens to the whole area of supporting student writing and what they recorded as the predominance of a study skills model, based on the presupposition both that language was a transparent medium of representation and that writing was a transferable skill (see Lea & Street, 1998). In challenging this approach, researchers made visible issues of power and authority around writing for assessment; this went beyond either developing generic writing skills or acculturating students into disciplinary writing practices. They foregrounded an academic literacies approach to student writing, examining issues of meaning making and identity and pointing to the requirement for students to switch between many different types of written text as they encountered new modules or courses and the implicit writing demands of different disciplinary genres, departments and, indeed, individual academic staff. Researchers have continued to unpack this diversity primarily through ethnographic-type qualitative case study research, looking at students' and academics' experiences of writing. The work starts from the position that literacy in the university is not a unitary skill that can be transferred with ease from context to context. A major focus of investigation remains the contested nature of text production, whatever the nature of these texts and the contexts within which a wide range of practices are instantiated. The approach has resonated with both practitioners and literacy researchers and, consequently, has been taken up across a range of contexts supporting student writers and also in relation to student learning more generally (Haggis, 2009). The field has always foregrounded the significance of paying attention to language in higher education and the implications of this for understanding and supporting teaching and learning not just student writing (Ivanič, 1998; Lea & Jones, 2011; Lea & Stierer, 2000; Lea and Street, 1998; Lillis, 2001; Thesen & van Pletzen, 2006; Turner, 2011). This includes interest in semiotic practice and multimodality across the different contexts of post-compulsory education (English, 2011; Ivanič et al., 2009) and aligns with a turn to semiosis in new and critical literacy studies more broadly (Kress, 2003; Williams, 2009).

During the last decade the field has expanded in a number of ways which are particularly important in relation to this chapter and its contribution to the volume overall. For example Lea (2004) outlines and explicates the principles of an approach to course design, based on the outcomes of academic literacies research, and the ways in which these might be implicated in practice. She illustrates these principles through the examination of a postgraduate online course, taken by practitioners working in post-compulsory education. More recent work has been concerned with new contexts for learning and more emphasis on the changing nature of higher education. For example, there has been more attention to writing in professional and vocational areas of study (Baynham, 2000; Rai, 2004) and postgraduate professional contexts (Lea, 2012) and consideration of the nature of literacies in a digital world (Goodfellow & Lea, 2007, 2013; McKenna & Hughes, 2013; Williams, 2009). In addition, there is increasing recognition that the academic literacies approach sits well alongside other relevant perspectives and, consequently, researchers are drawing in other theoretical and methodological approaches to their work. For example, both Hamilton (2011) and Lea (2013) are drawing on actor network theory; Coleman (2012) and Paxton and Frith (2013) use Bernsteinian theorisation of knowledge structures alongside academic literacies.

Despite these developments, we continue to claim that the value of an academic literacies focus is that it foregrounds the instantiation of literacy practices across the different contexts of higher education. That is, we would always see literacy in context rather than captured in a specific literacy curriculum. In the case study explicated below one of the authors of this chapter, Lynn Coleman, explores the detailed workings of literacy in relation to vocational higher education contexts. As global higher education shifts increasingly towards professional programmes of study, Coleman's work illustrates how the professional/vocational domain and its characteristics, from outside the academy, become infused in the curriculum. She signals how meaning and learning in higher education are increasingly being expressed through literacies and textual forms other than written language (Thesen & van Pletzen, 2006). This is partly a consequence of the expansion of vocational and professional courses, which has led to the reframing of what counts as knowledge in the academy (Ivanič and Lea, 2006; Lea, 2012). These changes have particular implication for the literacy practices that are given status or gain dominance in the HE context. Lea (2013) argues that the ways in which students are asked to demonstrate knowledge through the assignment texts they produce and the associated literacy practices these texts foreground are also being reframed. Within contemporary vocational higher education settings assignment texts that bear a direct resemblance to the types of textual products produced in professional practice are increasingly becoming prominent (Coleman, 2012; Pardoe, 2000; Rai, 2004). This might stem from the acceptance that in vocationally oriented courses the curriculum actively attempts to engage students with the kind of professional practices associated with their future careers (see Pardoe, 2000). These professionally relevant texts place less reliance on the written forms and practices that were once dominant in higher education (Lea & Stierer, 2000). For example, in the visual communication and media industries, such as film production, with a strong visual and multimodal basis the primary textual form is the audio-visual film. Academic literacies researchers exploring course environments using alternative forms of assignment types and texts have, however, pointed to the tensions that teachers and students have to manage when their course environments rely on the production of both written and non-written assignment texts (Archer, 2006; Mitchell et al., 2000; Thesen, 2001).

While some researchers using an academic literacies perspective have explored and provided insight into how the curriculum and pedagogic approaches have been able to harness and embrace the multimodal affordances of different textual practices (Archer, 2006; Mitchell et al., 2000) limited attention has been directed towards the influence of the actual vocational or professional educational context on the types of practices and texts privileged. A key contribution of academic literacies research has shown that the essay or essayist literacy is a privileged or dominant literacy practice in HE (Lillis, 2001). Lillis argues that the essay is 'really institutionalised shorthand for a particular way of constructing knowledge which has come to be privileged within the academy' (2001:20). While essayist literacy might be a dominant form of literacy practice in HE there is increasing recognition by academic literacies researchers that it also sits alongside other multimodal textual practices (Archer, 2006; Lea, 2008; Thesen, 2006). A further feature of academic literacies research is its primary focus on the actual individual practices of teachers and students, usually explored through the individuals' perspective of their own text production (see Tuck's (2012) research on teacher feedback and Lea & Jones, 2011). This focus on personal accounts of practice can make it harder to recognise and understand broader institutional or sectoral aspects. This has led to calls from within the field of academic literacies to widen the literacies lens to more suitably attend to institutional practices, particularly in new or unfamiliar learning contexts of higher education (Lea, 2013). In addition, in order to gain insights into how the professional context is implicated in curriculum and make sense of the relationship between literacy and curriculum we may need to extend our analytical lens.

With regard to the latter, Coleman's research has shown the value of incorporating a conceptual framework able to theorise knowledge and the curriculum alongside an academic literacies perspective – expanding the theoretical reach to include the broader higher education context. While the influence of this broader context has been acknowledged as important to the work of academic literacies researchers (see for example Lea, 2004; Lea & Street, 1998; Thesen and van Pletzen, 2006; Tuck, 2013), it has nonetheless been an area that has been under-theorised, with researchers' efforts typically focused more on individual institutional dynamics rather than on the sector more broadly.

## Recontextualisation in a vocational curriculum context

Using examples from film production and graphic design, Coleman's study explores how the curriculum in vocational higher education promotes certain industry-valued assumptions, knowledge and practices that then become embedded in the literacy practices associated with assignment production. The approach she took in her study integrated a literacy as social practice perspective with Basil Bernstein's (1975, 1996, 2000) theories of curriculum and knowledge recontextualisation. These two analytical lenses, one of literacy practice and the other of recontextualisation, were brought to bear on the assignment production processes of two visual communication and media courses at a South African vocational higher education institution. Her analytic approach looks in two directions – towards the literacy practices and recontextualisation processes – and offers insight into how the professional contexts and their privileged values and knowledge become implicated in the curriculum decision making, and are at the same time reflected in the literacy practices associated with teachers' and students' assignment processes and texts. Bernstein's theoretical concepts and intellectual project are most commonly associated with research focused on the schooling sector. However, this work has also been used in both theoretical and empirical ways to understand, describe and deconstruct disciplinary knowledge, curriculum formation and pedagogic organisation and structures within higher education settings (Ashwin, 2009; Czerniewicz, 2008; Maton, 2009; Moore, 2004; Shay, 2011, 2012; Vorster, 2008). Bernstein's (2000) concept of recontextualisation describes the process through which knowledge produced outside the educational context (in the disciplines or in professional environments) become transformed, adapted and re-appropriated to become subjects in the curriculum (Shay, 2011; Wheelahan, 2010). However, as this knowledge moves from its 'original site to its new positioning, as pedagogic discourse, a transformation takes place' (Bernstein, 2000:32). This transformation is ideologically mediated and as a result the knowledge from the original site of production is abstracted from its 'social base, position and power relations' (2000:38). An important outcome of this process is that the knowledge embedded in the subjects of any given curriculum is different from what might be called disciplinary or workplace knowledge (Muller, 2008). The curriculum in its broadest sense is thus an instantiation of recontextualisation processes (Shay, 2011; Singh, 2002) and reflects the mediated choices of curriculum role players, who in higher education are most likely to be subject lecturers.

By analysing the recontextualisation processes, the provenance of knowledge and practices and how they have been reconfigured and transformed into course content and assignment topics and tasks can be identified. This in turn provides a means of understanding why and how certain literacy practices are given value in the specific course environment. The curriculum is therefore conceptualised as an important site through which the social and cultural values and conventions of the course are communicated to students. Incorporating both an academic literacies perspective and recontextualisation theorisation offers a means of centring the student learning experience while also investigating the curriculum and its influence on learning.

In traditional universities the curriculum typically results from the recontextualisation of knowledge drawn primarily from the disciplines. However, in vocational higher education settings the recontextualisation processes that guide curriculum decision making are more complex (Wheelahan, 2008). Janus, the figure who 'looks' or 'faces' both ways, is often used as a metaphor to describe how vocational curricula have to accommodate disciplinary and professional demands in a bid to ensure the relevance, credibility and legitimacy of the courses on offer (Barnett, 2006; Gamble, 2006; Wheelahan, 2008). Barnett (2006) provides an explanation of recontextualisation in vocational environments. He explains that such curricula have to include knowledge specific to the practicalities of the profession, but also refer to bodies of knowledge that bear no direct relevance to that profession. When vocational curricula 'look both ways' – in the direction of professional and disciplinary fields – the moral order and foregrounded knowledge and practices of these distinct fields of practice and knowledge act to provide regulative frameworks that guide and, sometimes, dictate the recontextualisation processes associated with knowledge selection. A key characteristic of universities of technology, which represents the vocational higher education sector in South Africa, is its clear foregrounding and positioning of an 'education for employment' agenda (Du Pré, 2010; Winberg, 2005). This preparation for industry places a premium on the development of relevant skills and competencies required in professional practice and can be seen as an additional influence alongside the professional and disciplinary directives. It acts as a regulative framework which determines in very concrete ways how course content is selected in university of technology contexts. Muller uses the term 'contextual coherence' to describe curricula where the logic guiding curriculum decision making and recontextualisation is primarily derived from the logic of 'a particular specialised form of practice' (2009:216). In such curricula the decision to include particular content segments are premised on the assumption that it is useful in developing necessary understanding and skills demanded in industry (Muller, 2009). Relevance and value to professional practice is thus the primary factor determining what content is included in the curriculum.

In the case study below, Coleman describes a film production course at a South African university of technology and illustrates the factors influencing the recontextualisation process and its impact on the course curriculum. The case study shows that the underlying logic of the curriculum is primarily guided by a need to ensure coherence with the skill, knowledge and competency needs of the film production industry. This overt orientation towards professional practice means that the literacy practices associated with assignment production tend to privilege those that have legitimacy in professional practice. A major implication of this privileging of professionally relevant literacy texts and practices is the 'marginalisation' of other texts and practices such as those associated with disciplinary domains, such as Film Studies.

## Case study: film production

The film production case study was part of a larger ethnographic study undertaken at a South African university of technology exploring the assignment production practices in a film production and graphic design course. Guided primarily by the participant observation of the daily activities of teachers and students a range of interactional, documentary and textual artefact in visual, audio–visual, written and digital formats were also collected. The film production course had a student cohort of roughly 85 students and most of the 11 staff had strong ties to the local film industry. At the time of the study many were involved in various film production projects. These strong ties to the film industry were regarded as a key strength of the course and reflected the dominant vocational education ethos promoted at institutional level. Teachers and students perceived the course aims to be vocationally driven, thus the primary focus of the course was to prepare students for entry and employment in the film production industry. Adhering to this focus, the curriculum content and organisation explicitly sought to provide students with sufficient opportunities to development the necessary skills and competencies aligned to the specific roles and functions associated with professional film production. Both students and teachers communicated a very clear understanding of the industry relevance agenda as Dylan the course co-ordinator expresses: '[it] provide(s) them with *all the skills that make a filmmaker*. Directing, producing, lighting, camera, research skills, scriptwriting skills. Students have to be *competent in all those fields of filmmaking*.' The course co-ordinator's viewpoint was echoed by Neil, a Level 3 student, when he said:

> The *course equips us with necessary skills* . . . I know how to use a camera, I know how to write a script, I know where to go out looking for actors, doing my paper work and stuff like that. I could make it happen.

### Recontextualisation processes impacting on the film production curriculum

A primary characteristic of the course curriculum is the almost direct adoption and transposition of the Film Production Process, a structuring mechanism central to professional film making. In the film industry this process not only structures all aspects of the film production, but it is used as shorthand for the industry's different professional roles and responsibilities, which are also linked to the different stages of the film making process. In the film production course the Film Production Process acts as the main curriculum organisation and structuring tool. The subject naming, conventions and nature of the content taught in each subject and, importantly, the kinds of assignments students are required to produce are directly influenced by this process. In many ways this process also acts as a type of socialisation mechanism. Thus within the course the Film Production Process acts as a means whereby students are inducted into specifics way of making films which has relevance in the local film industry. This is further reinforced over the three-year course by assignments that require students to provide evidence and produce documentation that adhere to the sequencing of the Film Production process and undertake tasks specific to the different stages of the process. These assessments also evaluate whether students are developing skills and competencies associated with different roles and functions particular to the different stages of the film production process. The centrality of the Film Production Process in overseeing students' day-to-day academic activities, and that also feed into their assessment practices, is brought into sharp focus when visiting the Level 1 classroom as a large poster depicting the process dominates the notice board of this venue (see Figure 5.1) where most lectures take place.

Although the Film Production Process is a central influence on the curriculum decision making in the film course, the recontextualisation processes highlight how fractures and dislocations occur as the knowledge and practices from industry become transformed into the curriculum. While the syllabi and

*Figure 5.1* Poster outlining the film production process

subjects map, to some extent, onto the four stages of the film industry process, some areas of contrast and dislocation suggest that this industry-based process is not seamlessly transposed into the curriculum of the Film course. For instance, in industry the Film Production Process delineates fairly compartmentalised and sequential sets of activities and practices undertaken in each stage. This is particularly evident in the production of big budget films which often have a very rigid segmentation of tasks and activities. Practicalities specific to the academic environment of the course (i.e. the prescriptions associated with subject naming or the need to keep the number of subjects within a reasonable range) tend to blur the content boundaries of certain subjects and their relation to the stages of the Film Production Process. Figure 5.2 illustrates the recontextualised version of the Film Production Process and suggests how the subjects in the course curriculum are mapped onto the different phases of the Film Production Process. Some subjects directly align with different phases in the process, for example, Production Practice (Set Design) in the pre-production phase, and Digital Cinematography in the Production phase. However, there are points of disconnection and overlap, a consequence of the recontextualisation processes and curriculum decision making specific to the Film course. An example of a disconnection resulting from somewhat artificial restrictions imposed by the strongly controlled subject naming prescriptions, is that scriptwriting is accommodated under the subject Production Practice (see Figure 5.2). This implies that the activities of scriptwriting are aligned to the Production stage of the Film Production Process, even though in industry scriptwriting would more typically be part of the Development stage. These examples serve to highlight the characteristic features of the recontextualisation process, which involves the transformation and often reformulation of knowledge from its site of production into the academic environment in the form of curriculum. It is this characteristic feature which has lead scholars to suggest that educational or pedagogic knowledge as presented in the curriculum is distinctly different from professional or disciplinary knowledge (Muller, 2008). This example also illustrates the degree to which various constraints specific to the academic context also impact on the recontextualisation processes and results in the very context-specific reorganisation of knowledge and practices from industry into the curriculum.

Coleman's study illustrates the consequence of these recontextualisation processes on assignment production and the privileging of particular literacy practices. In her investigation of the Film curriculum, a clear differentiation emerged between knowledge, skills and practices associated with industry and those aligned more closely with disciplinary or academic environments. The recontextualised version of the Film Production Process as represented in Figure 5.2 shows evidence of this separation. Assignment texts in the course and their underpinning literacy practices also reflect this separation. There are clear distinctions in the nature of assignment production required in subjects that recontextualised the knowledge and practices of either the Film

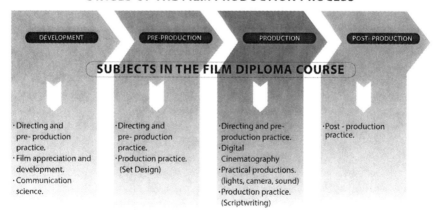

*Figure 5.2* Recontextualised stages of the film production process into subjects in film course

Production Process or those that have a stronger disciplinary affiliation like Film Appreciation and Development and Communication Science. In this course the participants understand this separation through their use the labels of 'theoretical' and 'practical' which serve to differentiate subjects from each other. Film Appreciation and Development and Communication Science which are only offered on Levels 1 and 2 of the course, are assigned a 'theory subject' label by course participants. In the course curriculum these subjects are recontextualised as part of the Development stage of the Film Production Process. In this way the disciplinary basis linked to media and communication theory and film history and analysis which form the core content of these subjects becomes part of the recontextualised Film Production Process. Subjects linked directly to the tasks and activities associated with the physical act of film production (typically associated with the Pre-production, Production and Post-production stages) are in turn assigned the 'practice' label.

> Film appreciation and development . . . is *just theory*. They watch movies and they write about it. So there's *no practical work in it*, they don't pick up a camera, they just watch and write and read. It is *pure theory* . . . Communication Science is also just pure theory. They don't make anything, they make posters to get a point across, but don't make any movies . . . those two subjects I would say are . . . purely *theoretical*.
>
> (Dylan, course co-ordinator)

In the above extract Dylan relies on the labels 'theoretical', 'just theory' or 'pure theory' to describe the Film Appreciation and Development and Communication Science subjects. He also suggests that these subjects involve 'no practical work'. For Dylan, theoretical subjects are therefore dislocated from practical work and the activities of making films. Anna, a Level 2 student, offers a similar insight into the nature of the Film Appreciation and Development subject, distinguishing it from the other 'more practical' subjects she is required to do in her course:

> A lot of the other subjects are *more practical* and *this subject is the only subject where we have to sit down*. You actually *have to do essays on an on-going basis* . . . Communication Science as well, ja. *Those are the two* . . . *writing-heavy subjects*, ja.

In the above extract Anna also links Film Appreciation and Communication Science with essays, suggesting that this is a 'theory subject' so is more concerned with written activities and essay writing.

When asked to elaborate on what 'practical' means in the course Dylan says that it is about '*making films,* . . . *doing anything that one of the major roles in the filmmaking process would actually do*. So scriptwriting would be writing a script, lighting would be putting up lights, etc. So that's how I see "*practical*"'.

In the Film course practical subjects are directly associated with the tasks and activities undertaken as part of the act of filmmaking. However, another way of conceptualising the distinction between practical and theoretical subjects in the course is with respect to what students are required to do as part of their classroom and assignment practices and the types of texts associated with these practices. Theoretical subjects typically require students to demonstrate their learning via written textual forms, for example, tests, essays, posters or classroom presentations. The assignment overview of the Film Appreciation and Development subject (Figure 5.3) shows how essays and tests are the primary assessment method used in this theoretical subject.

These texts and the underpinning literacy practices that guide their production are associated with the academic context rather than those that have legitimacy in the film industry. The assignments that students have to produce in their practical subjects are closely aligned to the act or process of making a

| ASSESSMENT OVERVIEW FOR THE YEAR WITH MARK ALLOCATIONS | |
|---|---|
| **TERM 1:** | |
| **ASSESSMENT 1:** | ESSAY 1: With reference to scenes from Monsoon Wedding, discuss how the director moved away from traditional Indian Cinema to make a globally competitive film. (50%) |
| **ASSESSMENT 2:** | ESSAY 2: Select one of the stories in the movie Amores Peros and discuss how the director was able to take an everyday story and make it a moving film. (50%) <br> **20% of year mark** |
| **TERM 2:** | |
| **ASSESSMENT 3:** | ESSAY 3: With reference to scenes from the film The Gods Must be Crazy, discuss how the Khoi people were portrayed in a derogative manner. (33.3%) |
| **ASSESSMENT 4:** | ESSAY 4: With reference to scenes from the film The Battle of The Algiers, discuss why the film was and still is used as a reference point for combat purpose by Army generals the world over. (33.3%) |
| **ASSESSMENT 5:** | EXAM (33.3%) - 1st SEMESTER WORK <br> **30% of year mark** |
| **TERM 3:** | |
| **ASSESSMENT 6:** | ESSAY 5: Discuss the success of the film Mapantsula, in spite of being censured in South Africa. (50%) |
| **ASSESSMENT 7:** | ESSAY 6: With reference to the scenes from the film Drum and other sources, discuss the advantages and disadvantages of casting international actors in SA films. (50%) <br> **20% of year mark** |
| **TERM 4:** | |
| **ASSESSMENT 8:** | ESSAY 7: Among other sources, use scenes from the film Tsotsi to discuss the challenges faced by post apartheid filmmakers. (40%) |
| **ASSESSMENT 9:** | EXAM - 2nd SEMESTER WORK (60%) <br> **30% of year mark** |

*Figure 5.3* Assignment overview for Film Appreciation and Development subject

film product. These assignments typically ask students to demonstrate skills or technical abilities associated with particular roles and function integral to the film making process. The assignment texts students have to produce are those that have currency and legitimacy in the film industry. Some of the assignment texts students produced included hand-drawn storyboards, floor plans, the construction of model sets and digital film clips and require students to use the specialist film technologies and software (see Figures 5.4 and 5.5).

The description of the assignment production practices in the film production course, when considered through both a literacy practice and recontextualisation lens, helps to make visible the relationship between curriculum and the nature of assignment texts that are clearly valued. The case illustrates how distinctions between the type of assignment texts students are required to produce and the literacy practices involved in their production are dependent on whether the underpinning knowledge being demonstrated has its provenance in professional practice or the discipline of Film Studies. In this course texts and literacy practices associated with the film industry are accommodated within the practical subjects, while those aligned to disciplinary contexts are assigned to the theory subjects. The recontextualised Film Production Process is assigned a prominent role in the curriculum and further functions at a pedagogic level to socialise students into ways of being associated with the film industry. This central curriculum and pedagogic role signals powerfully the foregrounding of an industry relevance agenda. The recontextualisation process means that theory subjects are located within the Film Production Process, which is both

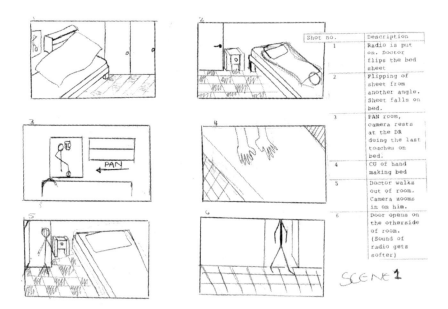

Figure 5.4 A storyboard produced for a short film

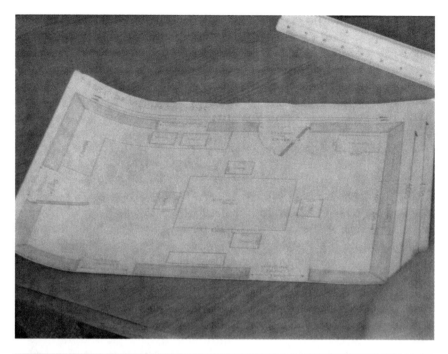

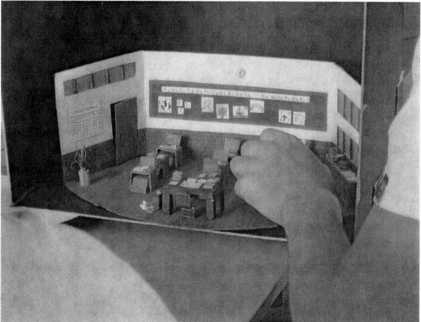

*Figure 5.5* Floor plans and a model set construction

a strategic and somewhat artificial means of creating or buying credibility for these disciplinary based theory subjects within the curriculum. As a result the literacy practices privileged in these subjects take on generic forms. This could be a consequence of the marginal position assigned to the theoretical subjects in the curriculum and the subsequent underdevelopment of a distinct disciplinary footprint associated with these subjects. As a result the written literacy practices which the curriculum and assignment requirements of these subject privileged rely rather heavily on decontextualised and generic conceptualisations of academic writing, particularly essay writing.

## Concluding comments

This chapter has been concerned with further expanding the academic literacies frame to take full account of the changing nature of the higher education curriculum and, more specifically, associated assessment practices. It illustrates how attention to aspects of vocational and professional curricula practices may reprioritise some aspects of the academic literacies work and also help to align it generatively with other theoretical lenses. In this respect, the case study illustrates how a recontextualisation lens allows for a further and more nuanced degree of visibility in our understanding of the roots of textual practices. As an analytic tool it helps make the detail of the curriculum more explicit, particularly in relation to the emerging vocational and professional contexts in higher education, similar to that discussed here. This orientation links to the more general argument made by academic literacies researchers concerning the contextual and situated nature of learning and textual practice; this illuminates the gaps that are frequently evident between teacher and students' interpretations of assessment tasks. The broader point that we are making here is that, across the HE curricula, we need to scrutinise explicitly how assignment texts and practices are implicitly fashioned by the different domains of professional or disciplinary knowledge. This awareness of knowledge types, how they have been brought into being and are articulated within different domains is key to any development of what we might term a literacy curriculum in higher education.

## References

Archer, A., 2006. Change as additive: Harnessing students' multimodal semiotic resources in an engineering curriculum. In L. Thesen & E. van Pletzen, (Eds). *Academic literacy and the languages of change*. London: Continuum, pp. 130–150.

Ashwin, P., 2009. *Analysing teaching-learning interactions in higher education: Accounting for structure and agency*. London: Continuum.

Barnett, M., 2006. Vocational knowledge and vocational pedagogy. In M. Young & J. Gamble, (Eds). *Knowledge, curriculum and qualifications for further education*. Cape Town: HSRC Press, pp. 143–158.

Baynham, M., 2000. Academic writing in new and emergent discipline areas. In M. R. Lea & B. Stierer, (Eds). *Student writing in higher education: New contexts*. Buckingham: SRHE/ Open University Press, pp. 17–31.

Bernstein, B., 1975. *Class, codes and control. Vol 3. Towards a theory of educational transmissions.* London: Routledge.

Bernstein, B., 1996. *Pedagogy, symbolic control and identity: theory, research, critique.* London: Taylor & Francis.

Bernstein, B., 2000. *Pedagogy, symbolic control, and identity: theory, research, critique.* Revised edition, Lanham and Oxford: Rowman & Littlefield.

Coleman, L., 2012. Incorporating the notion of recontextualisation in academic literacies research: the case of a South African vocational web design and development course. *Higher Education Research & Development,* 31(3): 325–338.

Czerniewicz, L., 2008. The field of educational technology through a Bernsteinian lens. In International Basil Bernstein Symposium, Cardiff University, 9–12 July.

Du Pré, R., 2010. Universities of technology in the context of the South African higher education landscape. In R. Townsend, (Ed). *Universities of technology: Deepening the debate.* Pretoria: Council on Higher Education, pp. 1–41.

English, F., 2011. *Student writing and genre. Rethinking academic knowledge.* London: Continuum.

Gamble, J., 2006. Theory and practice in vocational curriculum. In M. Young & J. Gamble, (Eds). *Knowledge, curriculum and qualifications for further education.* Cape Town: HSRC Press, pp. 87–103.

Goodfellow, R. & Lea, M. R., 2007. *Challenging e-learning in the university,* Maidenhead: SRHE & Open University Press.

Goodfellow, R. & Lea, M.R., 2013. Introduction: literacy, the digital, and the university. In R. Goodfellow & M.R. Lea, (Eds). *Literacy in the digital university: critical perspectives on learning, scholarship and technology.* London and New York: Routledge, pp. 1–14.

Haggis, T., 2003. Constructing images of ourselves? A critical investigation into 'approaches to learning' research in higher education. *British Educational Research Journal,* 29(1): 89–104.

Haggis, T., 2009. What have we been thinking of? A critical overview of 40 years of student learning research in higher education. *Studies in Higher Education,* 34(4): 377–390.

Hamilton, M., 2011. Unruly practices: what a sociology of translations can offer to educational policy analysis. *Journal of Educational Philosophy and Theory, Special Issue on Actor Network Theory* 43(S1): 55–75.

Ivanič, R., 1998. *Writing and identity. The discoursal construction of identity in academic writing.* Amsterdam: John Benjamins.

Ivanič, R. & Lea, M.R., 2006. New contexts, new challenges: the teaching of writing in the UK higher education. In L. Ganobcsik-Williams, (Ed). *Teaching academic writing in UK higher education.* Houndmills: Palgrave Macmillian, pp. 6–15.

Ivanič, R., Edwards, R., Barton, B., Martin-Jones, M., Fowler, Z., Hughes, B., et al., 2009. *Improving learning in college. Rethinking literacies across the curriculum.* Abingdon: Routledge.

Kress, G., 2003. *Literacy in the new media age.* London: Routledge

Lea, M. R., 2004. Academic literacies: a pedagogy for course design. *Studies in Higher Education,* 29(6): 739–756.

Lea, M. R., 2008. Academic literacies in theory and practice. In B. V. Street & N. H. Hornberger, (Eds). *Encyclopedia of language and education.* 2nd Edition, 2: Literacy, New York: Springer Science, pp. 227–238.

Lea, M. R., 2012. New genres in the academy: Issues of practice, meaning making and identity. In M. Castelló & C. Donahue, (Eds). *University writing: Selves and texts in academic societies.* Bingley: Emerald Group Publishing Limited, pp. 93–109.

Lea, M. R., 2013. Reclaiming literacies: competing textual practices in a digital higher education. *Teaching in Higher Education,* 18(1): 106–118.

Lea, M. R. & Jones, S., 2011. Digital literacies in higher education: exploring textual and technological practice. *Studies in Higher Education*, 36(4): 377–393.

Lea, M. R. & Stierer, B., 2000. Editors' introduction. In M. R. Lea & B. Stierer, (Eds). *Student writing in higher education. New contexts*. Buckingham: SRHE and Open University, pp. 1–13.

Lea, M. R. & Street, B. V., 1998. Student writing in higher education: An academic literacies approach. *Studies in Higher Education*, 23(2): 157–172.

Lillis, T., 2001. *Student writing: access, regulation, desire*. London: Routledge.

Lillis, T. & Scott, M., 2007. Defining academic literacies research: issues of epistemology, ideology and strategy. *Journal of Applied Linguistics*, 4(1): 5–32.

Maton, K., 2009. Cumulative and segmented learning: exploring the role of curriculum structures in knowledge-building. *British Journal of Sociology of Education*, 30(1): 43–57.

McKenna, C & Hughes, J., 2013. Values, digital texts, and open practices: A changing scholarly landscape in higher education In R. Goodfellow & M.R. Lea, (Eds). *Literacy in the digital university: Critical perspectives on learning, scholarship and technology*. London and New York: Routledge, pp. 15–26.

Mitchell, S., Marks-Fisher, V., Hale, L., & Harding, J., 2000. Making dances, making essays: Academic writing in the study of dance. In M. R. Lea & B. Stierer (Eds). *Student writing in the university: New contexts*. Buckingham: SRHE and Open University Press, pp. 86–96.

Moore, R., 2004. Responding to market and society. Curriculum challenges in a South African business school. Unpublished study prepared for the South African Universities Vice Chancellor's Association. Cape Town.

Muller, J., 2008. In search of coherence: A conceptual guide to curriculum planning for comprehensive universities. Report prepared for the SANTED Project. Centre for Educational Policy.

Muller, J., 2009. Forms of knowledge and curriculum coherence. *Journal of Education and Work*, 22(3): 205–226.

New London Group, 2000. A pedagogy of multiliteracies. Designing social futures. In B. Cope & M. Kalantzis, (Eds). *Multiliteracies*. London: Routledge, pp. 9–36.

Pardoe, S., 2000. A question of attribution: the indeterminancy of 'learning from experience'. In M.R. Lea & B. Stierer, (Eds). *Student writing in higher education: new contexts*. Buckingham: SRHE and Open University Press, pp. 125–146.

Paxton, M. & Frith, V., 2013. Implications of academic literacies research for knowledge making and curriculum design. *Higher Education* DOI 10.1007/s10734-013-9675-z

Rai, L., 2004. Exploring literacy in social work education: a social practice approach to student writing. *Journal of Social Work Education*, 40(2): 149–162.

Shay, S., 2011. Curriculum formation: A case study from history. *Studies in Higher Education*, 36(3): 315–329.

Shay, S., 2012. Educational development as a field: are we there yet? *Higher Education Research & Development*, 31(3): 311–323.

Singh, P., 2002. Pedagogising knowledge: Bernstein's theory of the pedagogic device. *British Journal of Sociology of Education*, 23(4): 571–582.

Thesen, L., 2001. Modes, literacies and power: a university case study. *Language and Education*, 15(2): 132–145.

Thesen, L., 2006. Who owns this image? Word, image and authority in the lecture. In L Thesen & E. van Pletzen, (Eds). *Academic literacy and the languages of change*. London: Continuum, pp. 151–179.

Thesen, L., & Van Pletzen, E., 2006. Introduction: The politics of place in academic literacy work. In L. Thesen & E. van Pletzen, (Eds). *Academic literacy and the languages of change*. London: Continuum, pp. 1–29.

Tuck, J., 2012. Feedback-giving as social practice: teachers' perspectives on feedback as institutional requirement, work and dialogue. *Teaching in Higher Education*, 17(2): 209–221.

Tuck, J., 2013. An exploration of practice surrounding student writing in the disciplines in UK higher education from the perspectives of academic teachers. Unpublished PhD thesis. Milton Keynes: The Open University.

Turner, J., 2011. *Language in the academy: Cultural reflexivity and intercultural dynamics*. London: Multilingual Matters.

Wheelahan, L., 2008. An analysis of the structure of curriculum in vocational qualifications in Australian tertiary education: how does it mediate access to knowledge? 5th International Basil Bernstein Symposium, Cardiff University, 9–12 July.

Wheelahan, L., 2010. *Why knowledge matters in curriculum. A social realist argument*, London: Routledge.

Williams, B., 2009. *Shimmering literacies: Popular culture and reading and writing online*, New York: Peter Lang.

Winberg, C., 2005. Continuities and discontinuities in the journey from technikon to university of technology. *South African Journal of Higher Education*, 19(2): 189–200.

Vorster, J.A., 2008. An analysis of curriculum development processes in a Journalism and Media Studies Department at a South African University. 5th International Basil Bernstein Symposium, Cardiff University, 9–12 July.

# Chapter 6

# Information literacy in the workplace

## Generic and specific capabilities

*Mark Hepworth*

## Introduction

This chapter is a personal reflection on the importance of and need for work-place information literacy based on twenty years of experience researching people's information behaviour and information literacy (also known as infor-mation skills, information capability, information competency, information capability, information management capability), as well as training people to be information literate. In particular the chapter was influenced by projects, over the last five years, which explored people's information behaviour and developed capabilities in the local government context, including health and social services.

Working in different domains and trying to understand people's informa-tion experience and factors affecting that experience, as well as looking at ways to enhance people's information capabilities, has highlighted tensions. In par-ticular there is a tension between recognising the socially embedded, context specific nature of learning (Lave & Wenger 1991; Lloyd 2011) and the desire to foster generic information capabilities. The latter has tended to lead to generic instruction that highlights commonalities across contexts that can, however, lead to a dislocation between the abstractions of the trainer and the reality of the learner. These 'commonalities' may be, for example, similar cognitive processes or procedures, exemplified by the numerous models of information literacy (Hepworth & Walton 2009, 2013) which do not correspond to the learners' lived experience. Models highlight various steps, processes and con-texts associated with: people becoming conscious of their information needs and defining these needs; their knowledge of their information environment and how to choose sources critically (informal and formal) and access sources effectively (people, places, objects, media). In addition they need to be com-petent at processing information and data (browse, synthesise, contrast, order etc.); manage the data and information (organising, storing, throwing away etc.) as well as building their own knowledge and, perhaps, sharing it with others. As a consequence this article identifies recognisable, high-level infor-mation capabilities experienced in the workplace which span contexts and yet notes their embedded nature and how different contexts may favour specific information capabilities. The article draws on examples of interventions that have enabled people to develop these capabilities in the workplace.

## Background

Most human activities are accompanied by artefacts that contain information and data. These artefacts may document activities, events and situations; what's been done (such as records of transactions or agreements) as well as strategies, explanations and guidelines etc. These capture, codify and share insights and help make sense of particular realities through symbols, texts and images and provoke dialogue. Learning about learning may be through published guidelines and instructions for handling information and data, for example, the *Information Sharing Guidance for Practitioners and Managers* (Department for Children, Schools and Families 2008) or corporate guidelines on information governance. Learning also takes place through doing, participation and action, within a context and with other people, where they share interpretations via dialogue and behave in certain ways that communicate ways of doing, norms and implicit values. For example in one context, such as a financial dealing environment, data and information is thought to be archival after a short space of time. In other environments where sensitive information about people is held privacy issues may influence how information is handled.

Managing learning and taking systematic approaches to using information and data and creating situations where learning and knowledge can be sensed and shared, to some extent, has always been important but is now given greater emphasis. This is partly due to the increase in the number of people involved in information-intensive activities that lead to the generation of data and information in a variety of media. This socio-technical context has resulted in a range of data and information processing tools, such as computers and applications that facilitate the creation, organisation, storage and use of data and information. Effective use of data and information, however, not only requires technology but depends on people's capabilities and, in particular, information capabilities that enable them to create, access, use, store and share information and data and, generally, participate in learning. Over the last twenty years these capabilities have been listed under various 'literacy' headings including: 'functional', 'digital', 'data', 'media' and 'information' literacy and broad inclusive terms such as 'transliteracy' (Hepworth & Walton 2009). They have been highlighted in a variety of contexts, such as in the health domain, for example, where they have been related to the life-long learning capability of nurses (Cheek & Doskatsch 1998). However, less attention has been paid to these capabilities in the workplace than in the educational context where information literacy has been linked to academic literacy that fosters 'good' academic practice and achieving academic success, and is associated with critical thinking and independent learning.

What does information literacy in the workplace mean? Choo (1996: 329) states that 'without a firm grasp of how it creates, transforms and uses information, an organisation would lack the coherent vision to manage and integrate its information processes, information resources and information technologies'. Choo goes on to explain why organisations need information: to enable decision making; make sense of changes in the external environment; and generate new knowledge. Implicit in these statements is the belief that people have the necessary capabilities to undertake these activities.

Broad generalisations and assumptions can be made about the nature of information literacy in the workplace. Some people in organisations need to be able to define the information that is needed to undertake either their own tasks or those of others. Senior staff tend to define needs whereas others may be told what to find out or what information to use (Hepworth & Smith 2008). For example, staff working in corporate communications may be asked to monitor certain sources of information and look for specific types of information, such as media coverage of their organisation. People in an organisation are therefore likely to need to be able to find information and use information to fulfil their role and, generally, make sense of what is happening around them. An emphasis on external information, such as news stories, company or market research, corporate web sites, legislation etc. tends to be associated with roles such as management consultancy, corporate finance or marketing where understanding the changing environment and new developments is vital and necessitates access to a broad range of external/environmental information. However, for many people greater emphasis may be placed on internal information systems and the use of primary data. This may involve the use of internal systems such as databases: applications such as Excel and project management software; the intranet or enterprise resource or content management systems. For example, administrators working in finance primarily use internal budgetary systems (Hepworth & Smith 2008). However, whether accessing and using external or internal information, employees need to know how to choose sources of information, how to use them (for example choosing appropriate terms, such as keywords, to search for information) and understand the functionality of, for example, information retrieval, storage or dissemination systems so that they can be used systematically to find or communicate appropriate information. Knowing what information is relevant, of sufficient breadth, depth or specificity or authority and hence being able to critically evaluate the information they find, as well the mechanistic skills of being able to sort, display, capture and manipulate retrieved information etc., are therefore important. It is also likely that these activities may be collaborative. For example, the evaluation of information and data may take place in conjunction with other people (Hepworth & Smith 2008) and is likely to reflect the socially embedded nature of these judgements and the value systems of the organisation.

Most people in the organisation would need to organise, or conform to ways of organising and storing information and data securely and in a way that enables others to access data and information. For example, this would include conforming to corporate file structures to store information or retention plans or archiving policy that help decide what to keep or throw away and how. For example, managing emails is one task that many people have to undertake (Hepworth & Smith 2008). People would need to conform to recognised good practice, for example, not storing information on memory sticks that are easily lost or using secure systems to communicate sensitive information. Furthermore, depending on the tasks and the nature of the information generated there may be sensitivities and norms in terms of how data is handled, such as respecting privacy and complying with legislation such as the Data Protection Act. Dealing with information securely, including organising, storing and ensuring appropriate access, is an important capability. In the public sector, in particular, where a great deal of sensitive personal information is managed, organisations such as the Information Commission have raised the profile of information management and the consequences of poor information management by fining organisations that err. Employees therefore need to understand systems and practices for managing, organising and handling information securely.

The ability to process information and data and to ensure, in particular, the quality of the information or data is increasingly important. Good decisions tend to be made on the basis of good data/information. For example, in organisations where numerous information systems have evolved over the years or where organisations share systems, data entered by different people may not be accurate or compatible leading to duplication and errors and, hence, conformity to common standards is increasingly important. People therefore need to recognise the importance of data quality, how the information may be useful to others and the implications for effective storage.

To be able to access and communicate information and ideas is, of course, key among organisations such as consultants and strategists. Here critical, analytical skills are fundamental in order to critically evaluate and process (synthesise, compare, recognise patterns, discard etc.) information and data and use texts, images or oral information to make or enable others to make judgements, decisions or reach common conclusions. In addition, the ability to communicate information clearly and logically is important. For example, Barbara Minto's pyramid principal, breaking down issues into 'situation-complication-question-answer' (1987), has become a popular technique among management consultants, such as PA consulting, to help them clearly communicate ideas. The oral nature of much communication has not received a great deal of attention. However, Crosling and Ward (2002) have flagged the importance of oral communication skills and Searle (2002) highlights the importance of listening. These authors draw attention to the fact that textual (information) literacy, which tends to be the focus of authors who write about academic information literacy, is but one part of the information capability picture.

The sharing of information, a complex phenomenon which may be influenced by organisational culture, individual relationships and judgements that relate to trust and perceived benefit, has become particularly important where organisations collaborate over the delivery of services, such as local government agencies. Local government agencies, for example health services, the police, and adult and children's services, need to exchange information to help people in the community. However, the decision to share and how to share is complex. For example, in addition to knowing the mechanics of formulating information sharing agreements and what they can and cannot share and how to share information, employees need to know the benefits of sharing information. This may, for example, help to identify who to share with and lead to earlier intervention and avoid a problematic situation getting worse (or more costly) and may enable a multi-agency, joined-up approach to the provision of services. The importance of these issues is indicated by the numerous government projects concerning information sharing and the publication of guides, such as, *Information Sharing: Guidance for Practitioners and Managers* (Department for Children Schools and Families 2008). A fundamental component of information sharing is networking which has been highlighted as an important work-based literacy (Hepworth & Smith 2008; Hoyer 2010). Personal networks enable the gathering and dissemination of information and may also be used to help judge the quality of information and data through consultation with peers and experts. The ability to develop one's network is therefore a key information capability.

However, different people in various sectors and roles are likely to place more emphasis on specific information capabilities. For example, certain roles may be more demanding in terms of access to information, data and expertise. The role of a leader of an organisation tends to be information intensive and require data and information about the activities in the organisation, as well as about the operating environment. Sales and marketing people may need information about their competitors, clients, new products and the changing socio-economic environment to help understand the market or the needs of their clients. This would, for example, enable them to tailor their sales, marketing and support to these needs. Administrators would tend to be processing information generated by the activities of staff and clients. Manufacturers may need information about processes, procedures, materials, equipment and suppliers. To a lesser or greater extent financial literacy will also be important for a number of functionaries. The nature of roles and tasks will therefore result in differences in terms of the significance and value placed on different types of data and information and the impact that data and information will have. As a consequence people will place more or less emphasis on information seeking, processing and use. In other words information practices will vary depending on the context and the information culture. These practices are likely to be learnt through participating in practice and informal mentoring and training rather than as a result of formal data and information competency frameworks and professional training.

## Conclusion

People's information behaviour when working as part of a community of practice is therefore complex, socially constructed and involves a host of capabilities, attitudes and knowledge. In many organisations these tend to be learnt through practice, observation, trial and error, informal mentoring, dialogue and interaction with systems, information, data and people. One could argue that these capabilities (behaviours, attitudes, knowledge) can only be learnt though participation in the community since the motivation to 'learn' is primarily in relation to undertaking work-based tasks and becoming an active and valued participant in the community. It is also likely that the associated norms and values are implicit and seldom made explicit and are only evident or become absorbed through interaction and working with others. In other words we are dealing with an information culture. It is possible, however, to be proactive and bring these to the foreground of people's thinking and provide insights so that people can be enabled to approach information and data tactically. Nevertheless, personal experience of enhancing information literacy in the many environments has indicated that building people's information capacity needs to be closely linked to the desired affordances i.e., enabling people to make sense of their world and meet their immediate, as well as long-term, goals, rather than being taught in the abstract.

In many workplaces little emphasis is given to fostering people's capacity to create or exploit information. Generally, learning to be information literate within a particular community is an informal process, often by chance or trial and error and through 'osmosis'. Asking peers is the most likely learning strategy or perhaps being shown how to do an information task, such as how to complete an information sharing agreement. However, in some organisations information training does take place. For example, in the health service health workers are trained in evidence based medicine where they are taught how to evaluate the quality of information and, in the public sector, guidelines are provided to enable information governance (Health and Social Care Information Centre 2014).

Nevertheless, in general, people's information capabilities in the workplace have not been comprehensively addressed. Studies in the local government context indicated that there was a great deal of variation in people's knowledge of how to handle information and a lack of consistency (Hepworth 2013). Methods used to convey this type of knowledge have tended to be in the form of textual guidelines and, because of the generic style, not often linked to concrete examples or case studies that help people understand and apply these to real life situations. A more innovative approach needs to be taken to developing people's information capabilities/information literacies in the workplace. In fact there are many ways of learning, Crawford and Irving (2009) cite Gerber (1998) who identifies eleven ways to learn in the workplace. Crawford and Irving also make the point that not all learning is situated in the community of practice and that people may bring and apply previous experience from other contexts and can learn from formal sources. However, whatever the training, it is likely that training needs to be seen to relate to the trainees' work and be seen to enable them to undertake their work. For example, in the local government context although there were numerous documents describing the Data Protection Act, it was misunderstood. There were cases where employees refused to share information due to a fear of falling foul of the act, even though the interests of clients would have been served and would have been permissible (Hepworth 2013). In Leicestershire's County Council this has led to the development of an e-learning package in participation with staff from social services, the health service and the police (February 2014). The design of the package placed a great deal of emphasis on the rationale for sharing and the benefits of sharing information to help motivate sharing, in addition to covering the mechanics of what can and can be shared and how. Case studies were woven into the learning material to enable learners to relate information to their context. In addition, the Loughborough Art School has been commissioned to develop short animations where 'information characters' engage in situations where sharing can and should not take place. These will be used with teams. The brevity and also the inclusion of humour is hoped to encourage staff to engage with the stories and take on attitudes and behaviours that otherwise they may not. It is also expected that such interventions are likely to stimulate dialogue about information practice and hence help to bring information management to the foreground of people's thinking.

One of the challenges of fostering people's information capabilities is that information underpins almost every activity and that it so embedded that people's interaction with information is to a great extent unconscious. In general people are concerned with completing a task rather than thinking about the role information could or should play or who else would benefit from the information or how it should be stored. Thus persuading people to make the time to learn about 'learning' is challenging. One approach was seen in local government; it proved to be an effective way to help bring information management to the foreground of people's thinking and enable them to reflect on their information practices. In this case people who worked in a team were brought together to reflect on and discuss different stereotypical images (personas) of information behaviours. Three example personas, 'the greedy', 'the sharer' and 'the follower of procedure' are shown in Figure 6.1.

The outcome of this workshop was that team members became aware of the lack of common practice and the risks associated with certain information behaviours and the advantages of others. In other words their information behaviour was brought to the foreground of their thinking. Through discussion they were able to reach a consensus on 'good information practice'. Interestingly this was the first time these staff had had an opportunity to reflect on their information behaviour.

What is clear is that people's information capabilities in the workplace deserve greater attention and further research and for effective ways to develop these capabilities to be found and tested. There is, of course, a place for traditional training courses in, for example, the use of particular systems and guides provided. However, even here there is a need to ensure that training and

*Figure 6.1* Three example personas, 'the greedy', 'the sharer' and 'the follower of procedures'.

instruction is designed to focus on the outcome and impact of these capabilities i.e., the benefits of information management and what it enables people to do. Ideally these capabilities would be built into professional and organisational competency frameworks that indicate the skills, knowledge and attitudes that all staff, especially new staff, need to have. In addition, the author would also argue that information capabilities, such as those described above, could be encouraged and developed before people reach the workplace. For example, in schools and in higher education greater emphasis could be placed on developing information capabilities. This would enable learners to develop general information management capabilities that could be applied in a wide range of contexts in addition to the academic information literacies that tend to be the focus of information literacy interventions.

## References

Cheek, J. and Doskatsch, I. (1998). Information literacy: a resource for nurses as lifelong learners. *Nurse Education Today*, 18, pp. 243–250.

Choo, C. (1996). The knowing organisation: how organizations use information to construct meaning, create knowledge and make decisions. *International Journal of Information Management*, 16(5): 329–340.

Crawford, J. and Irving, C. (2009). Information literacy in the workplace: a qualitative exploratory study. *Journal of Librarianship and Information Science*, 41(1): 29–38.

Crosling, G. and Ward, I. (2002). Oral communication: the workplace needs and uses of business graduate employees. *English for Specific Purposes*, 21, 4–57.

Department for Children, Schools and Families. (2008). *Information sharing for practitioners and managers*. Nottingham: Department for Children, Schools and Families.

Gerber, R. (1998). How do workers learn in the workplace? *Journal of Workplace Learning*, 16(1–32): 22–33.

Health and Social Care Information Centre. (2014). Available online: http://systems.hscic.gov.uk/ last accessed 10 February 2014.

Hepworth, M. (2013). A study of the information behaviour of people working in local government: building corporate information capacity. Paper presented at the Information, Interactions and Impact (i3) conference, held at Robert Gordon University, Aberdeen, UK, 25–28 June 2013.

Hepworth, M. and Smith, M. (2008). Workplace information literacy for administrative staff in HE. *Australian Library Journal*, 57(3): 212–236.

Hepworth, M. and Walton, G. (2009). *Teaching information literacy for inquiry based learning*. Cambridge: Woodhouse Publishing.

Hepworth, M. and Walton, G. (2013). *Developing people's information capabilities: fostering information literacy in educational, workplace and community contexts*. Bingley, UK: Emerald Group Publishing.

Hoyer, J. (2010). Information is social: information literacy in context. *Reference Services Review*, 39(1): 10–23.

Lave, J. and Wenger, E. (1991). *Situated learning: legitimate peripheral participation*. New York: Cambridge University Press.

Lloyd, A. (2011). Trapped between a rock and a hard place: what counts as information literacy in the workplace and how is it conceptualized? *Library Trends*, 60(2): 277–296.

Minto, B. (1987). *The Pyramid Principle*. Harlow, UK: Pearson Education Limited.

Searle, J. (2002). Situated literacies at work. *International Journal of Education Research*. 37: 17–28.

# Chapter 7

# Repurposing information literacy for the twenty-first century

*John Crawford*

## Introduction

Fundamental to the understanding of information literacy is the concept of the information society, which is one in which the creation, distribution and treatment of information have become the most significant economic and cultural activities. The information society is often contrasted with societies which are primarily industrial or agrarian. While information literacy activity certainly takes place in agrarian and industrial societies, in an information society information is increasingly flowing through information and communications technology (ICT). While this greatly facilitates the transmission of information it also leads to confusion as to what is ICT activity and what is information activity. An information society also covers many related sectors which include industrial and economic policy, technology policy, telecommunications policy as well as a huge sector including: social issues and policies that comprise e-government, education, e-health, media policy and cultural issues within which much of the material of information literacy includes concepts such as meaning, knowledge, communication, truth and representation and mental stimulus (UNESCO 2009:123–124).

## Defining information literacy

Definitions and interpretations of information literacy are discussed below but a working introductory definition which is widely used is that proposed by the Chartered Institute of Library and Information Professionals (2004): 'Information literacy is knowing when and why you need information, where to find it, and how to evaluate, use and communicate it in an ethical manner'.

The term 'information literacy' was coined in 1974 by Paul Zurkowski (Zurkowski 1974) and its origins were not specifically located in higher education. Zurkowski used the phrase to describe the 'techniques and skills' known by the information literate 'for utilizing the wide range of information tools as well as primary sources in molding information solutions to their problems'. Zurkowski himself was founding president of the US Information Industries Association, a trade and industry association which represented the USA's leading print publishers. One advocacy strategy he employed was to insist that because information products and services, aided and abetted by the exploding ICT technologies, were beginning to multiply it was necessary for informed citizens and policy makers to become more 'literate' in their use of these information services and products. However, Zurkowski himself admitted that there was little understanding of what the term meant until about ten years after he had coined it (Horton 2011). Other writers at the time expanded the concept to include an instrument of political emancipation and a requirement for competiveness in organisations (Pinto et al. 2010). The 1980s was a transition decade characterised by the rapid development of ICT technologies and in particular the appearance of the first personal computers. A key early and enduring document is the American Library Association's *Presidential committee on information literacy: Final report* (ALA 1989). The committee outlined six principal recommendations:

1    to 'reconsider the ways we have organized information institutionally, structured information access, and defined information's role in our lives at home in the community, and in the work place';
2    to promote 'public awareness of the problems created by information illiteracy';
3    to develop a national research agenda related to information and its use;
4    to ensure the existence of 'a climate conducive to students' becoming information literate';
5    to include information literacy concerns in teacher education; and
6    to promote public awareness of the relationship between information literacy and the more general goals of 'literacy, productivity, and democracy'.

This wide ranging statement shows that a clear role was identified for information literacy in the workplace, lifelong learning and as a civil and civic right. However, the 1990s was a period when librarians became increasingly dissatisfied with traditional user education and began to search for a more meaningful and appropriate term for an age of increasingly self-directed learning and the term information literacy began to replace user education. It was also a period when information literacy became principally located in education and especially in higher education where the librarian became both its main advocate and also its proprietor. The new century has seem the internationalisation of the concept with increasing support from UNESCO which has resulted in two major international policy statements, the Prague Declaration (UNESCO 2003) and the Alexandria Proclamation (Garner 2005). These are major advocacy tools. The Prague Declaration outlined the following principles:

•    The creation of an Information Society is key to social, cultural and economic development of nations and communities, institutions and individuals in the 21st century and beyond.

- Information Literacy encompasses knowledge of one's information concerns and needs, and the ability to identify, locate, evaluate, organize and effectively create, use and communicate information to address issues or problems at hand; it is a prerequisite for participating effectively in the Information Society, and is part of the basic human right of lifelong learning.
- Information Literacy, in conjunction with access to essential information and effective use of information and communication technologies, plays a leading role in reducing the inequities within and among countries and peoples, and in promoting tolerance and mutual understanding through information use in multicultural and multilingual contexts.
- Governments should develop strong interdisciplinary programs to promote Information Literacy nationwide as a necessary step in closing the digital divide through the creation of an information literate citizenry, an effective civil society and a competitive workforce.
- Information Literacy is a concern to all sectors of society and should be tailored by each to its specific needs and context.
- Information Literacy should be an integral part of Education for All, which can contribute critically to the achievement of the United Nations Millennium Development Goals, and respect for the Universal Declaration of Human Rights.

These principles link information literacy to wider human rights issues, specifically links it to the information society, defines it and links it to civil rights, the closure of the digital divide, reduction of inequality and improvement in workplace performance. It also suggests that information literacy is not a fixed concept but 'should be tailored by each to its specific needs and context'.

The Alexandria Proclamation (2005) reiterates some of these points. Information literacy:

- comprises the competencies to recognise information needs and to locate, evaluate, apply and create information within cultural and social contexts;
- is crucial to the competitive advantage of individuals, enterprises (especially small and medium enterprises), regions and nations;
- provides the key to effective access, use and creation of content to support economic development, education, health and human services, and all other aspects of contemporary societies, and thereby provides the vital foundation for fulfilling the goals of the Millennium Declaration and the World Summit on the Information Society; and
- extends beyond current technologies to encompass learning, critical thinking and interpretative skills across professional boundaries and empowers individuals and communities.

It links information literacy strongly with critical thinking and goes on to urge links with lifelong learning.

Australia also sees information literacy in this light contributing to: 'learning for life; the creation of new knowledge; acquisition of skills; personal, vocational, corporate and organisational empowerment; social inclusion; participative citizenship; and innovation and enterprise' (Australian Library and Information Association 2006). Information literacy and lifelong learning are related concepts: they are both largely self-motivated and self-directed and do not need the mediation of an outsider, individual or corporate (assuming, of course, that the individual has the necessary knowledge and skills), they are both self-empowering and benefit everyone irrespective of social or economic status and there are both 'self-actuating' or self-enlightening processes especially if practiced over a lifetime (Horton 2008: 3–4).

Information literacy is therefore about personal and civil rights, participative citizenship, lifelong learning, using technology wisely, the reduction of the digital divide, skills and economic development, education and critical thinking and the maintenance of a healthy lifestyle.

How information literacy should be defined has been the subject of much scholarly debate (Bawden 2001). Paul Zurkowski described information literate people as: 'People trained in the application of information resources to their work . . . ' emphasising the importance of the workplace but in 1979 the US Information Industries Association widened the definition of an information literate person as someone who 'knows the techniques and skills for using information tools in molding solutions to problems' and C. S. Doyle (1994) succinctly defined it as 'the ability to access, evaluate and use information from a variety of sources', a definition which in various forms has survived ever since. However, by the early 1990s two factors had emerged which are crucial to this study: there was little agreement within the information profession about what information literacy actually was and there was little understanding of the concept outside the profession. There was also criticism of the idea as being too 'library centred' and that information should include films, television, posters, conversations etc. The coming of widespread use of the Internet in the 90s greatly strengthened this view. In 1989 the American Library Association (1989) offered a new definition:

> To be information literate an individual must recognise when information is needed and have the ability to locate, evaluate and use effectively the information needed . . . Ultimately information literate people are those who have learned how to learn. They know how to learn because they know how information is organised, how to find information, and how to use information in such a way that others can learn from them.

Despite attempts to broaden the definition of information literacy and make it less 'library centred' it became increasingly linked with formal education and was taken up enthusiastically by academic librarians who saw it as a natural progression from traditional bibliographic instruction and who, in the United

States, had seen a considerable expansion in student demand for training in information skills at the expense of reference services. However it is not clear to what extent this was a genuine policy change or simply a rebranding exercise. Information literacy in higher education also came to be linked with the idea of a hierarchy or 'laddering' of skills by which various levels of information skill were linked to successive levels of undergraduate and post graduate learning, a good example of which is the SCONUL Seven Pillars of Information Literacy (SCONUL 2011). This has led to dominance of the concept by academic and to a lesser extent by school librarians which has reinforced the 'library centred' model of information literacy as a skill imparted by and dominated by librarians and one which has an element of academic assessment. This has led to a focus on individual student performance and the development of self-sufficiency through independent learning. However, the debate is now widening thanks to a limited but growing interest in workplace and wider community studies although these, for the most part, are attempts to translate librarians' perceptions in relation to the operationalisation of a list of skills and standards derived from the education sector. There is little reflection on whether information skills appropriate to the education sector are valued by workers and their employers. It also appears to be accepted that information literacy focuses on individual information use rather than information use as a collective activity. In reality workers use other workers' embodied knowledge and experience as a source of evaluated information. Research suggests that the role of the community is central to information literacy practice and that information literacy is not a skill but a practice which takes place through a range of social activities. Information literacy is therefore to be understood as a collaborative and communal activity. To complicate matters further, the language used by the information sector does not mean much outside it, which means that, when the term 'information literacy' leaves its domain, it loses its power (Lloyd 2011: 279–283). Within the profession itself sectoral approaches tend to be dissimilar and specific to the needs of the sector. In the health sector, information literacy tends to be evidence based but in special libraries a more corporate approach may apply. Academics tend to be concerned with learning outcomes and pedagogy while public librarians are more concerned with social inclusion. A study of the use of the term in the published literature showed that 50 per cent of the documents analysed derived from the subject areas of information, education and computing. Business and management were insignificant areas (Pinto et al. 2010: 14). For those concerned with information literacy in relation to lifelong learning issues the previous emphasis on education, problems with definitions and authority outside the information world represent major challenges.

## The changing nature of information literacy

The changing nature of conceptions of information literacy can be understood by looking at two non-education sectors, the workplace and the public library.

There are few better descriptions of information literacy skills development in an educational setting than that provided by Annemaree Lloyd (2011: 280):

> The skills prescribed in searching for information, accessing and using it are formalized by particular rules, regulations and curriculums that are underpinned by an instrumental rationality. This allows the acquisition of knowledge to be measured against formalized sets of criteria. In this setting, primacy is awarded to knowledge that is canonical, objective, and explicit and there is a focus on individual performance and the development of self-sufficiency through independent learning.

It could also be said that it is a setting in which librarians award themselves the role of judge and arbiter. It is all very different in the workplace. Here task and problems tend to be messy, complex and open ended. They may be difficult to analyse. They may employ different approaches to information seeking and use that go beyond the mastery of information seeking skills to knowing ways of thinking and seeing. In the workplace tasks are context specific, not generic. The focus is less on identifying information needs because problems are very specific and may be assigned to an employee to resolve (Weiner 2011). Workplace information literacy activity is a collaborative experience. Rather than skills based, individual activity in the workplace information literacy is a collaborative and social activity. To quote Annemaree Lloyd again:

> . . . I have reconceptualized information literacy as a practice that facilitates a 'way of knowing' about the sources of information that will inform performance and participation. These information sources are not confined to textual sources but also physical and social sources that constitute an information landscape, producing an information experience that has embodied and social dimensions in addition to the cognitive. Consequently, I understand information literacy as being holistic.
>
> (2010: 89)

In the workplace the view of what information is, is different from education with its reliance on standardised print and online sources – books, journals, technical manuals, password protected bibliographic databases and Internet sources. There is less reliance on secondary and codified sources. Annemaree Lloyd, in her study of Australian firefighters (2009), found practitioners to be a critical source of information. She considers that information literacy should be extended to include bodily experiences like touch and smell; senses that we all uses to varying degrees but are critical in certain situations such as firefighters for gaining information. For her information literacy should be viewed as 'the catalyst for learning about work and professional practice'. In a study of workplace information usage in Glasgow (Crawford and Irving 2009) the principal source of information used by employees was found to be other staff. This is an entirely reasonable point of view. People can be evaluated as a source of information just like any other. Colleagues with appropriate qualifications, training, experience and who have the respect of their peers can reasonably be viewed as a reliable information source. It was also found that human relationships are key to development of information literacy in the workplace. The choice of Internet sites to view was also influenced by how colleagues view one another. Websites were accepted as reliable on the recommendation of staff respected by colleagues. Among other sources of information pressed into service were advisory leaflets produced by governments and information posted on notice boards. It is not surprising that, in such a world, the role of the librarian as an authority figure is much diminished.

Another key difference from education is the concept of 'laddered skills' as exemplified in frameworks such as the SCONUL Seven Pillars (SCONUL 2011) where a hierarchy of skill levels is established which are then linked or 'pegged' to educational and social policy documents, depending on the perceived needs of the situation. As indicated above the workplace situation is 'messy' and there are identifiable factors (Lloyd 2010: 75–76):

- Information seeking is not always necessary.
- Information seeking is by trial and error.
- Getting information is not equal to getting the answer.
- Information seeking is not linear.
- Information seeking is not a one man job.
- Information relevance criteria change.

However, there are some 'pegs' on which to hang skill levels. Senior staff engage in different information literacy activities from other staff. They use more primary sources such as internally generated information than the secondary sources that are important in academic work. For them networking is also a productive way of gathering information (Weiner 2011). There is something of a hierarchy in the workplace with staff in senior and management positions with degrees and similar qualifications having a more sophisticated grasp of what information literacy is and how to use information. This is particularly marked in the public sector where specific qualification levels are attributed to particular levels of work and where there is a culture of continuing professional development (CPD) and relevant skills training (Crawford and Irving 2009). The downside of this is that staff with low-level skills in manual or semi-skilled posts can be viewed as a sort of information literacy proletariat. Cooke and Greenwood (2008) found that job function is the most critical factor in determining whether employees will have reasonable workplace access to ICT. While manual staff are keen to learn, the attitude of line managers is crucial if skill levels are to progress beyond basic IT competency. The danger of a digital divide was one of the authors' main conclusions.

While information literacy is clearly a different beast from its educational equivalent, it does have something in common with another workplace ideology – knowledge management. Knowledge management is concerned with an individual's knowledge, much of which is tacit knowledge residing in people's heads:

> Knowledge management comprises a range of strategies and practices used in an organization to identify, create, represent, distribute, and enable adoption of insights and experiences. Such insights and experiences comprise knowledge, either embodied in individuals or embedded in organizational processes or practice. Knowledge management efforts typically focus on organizational objectives such as improved performance, competitive advantage, innovation, the sharing of lessons learned, integration and continuous improvement of the organization.
>
> (Wikipedia 2010)

Stuart Ferguson (2009) notes that while the sites of information may be broader in a workplace context than they are in a higher educational institution the focus remains on individual learning. Although it should be noted that the lessons from workplace information literacy studies show that whilst the learning itself is individual, information literacy workplace activity is generally collaborative. With knowledge management the focus is generally on the organisation's capacity to learn, not the individual's. However, as indicated above, traditional concepts of information literacy cannot be sustained in the work environment. Whilst information literacy and knowledge management have separate roots they increasingly have issues in common. As Lloyd (2009) highlights, information literacy 'pursues the same goals as knowledge management . . . which is to develop and nurture the knowledge sharing practices and information literate workforce that are necessary if organisations are to be adaptive, innovative and robust'. There are four significant areas of similarity between knowledge management and information literacy:

1   Both are inextricably linked in the minds of many people with learning – lifelong learning in the case of the individual, the learning organisation in the case of the organisation.
2   The arguments for developing information literacy and knowledge management capability within the workplace/organisation are indisputable. Very few senior managers deny the benefits of managing and using the organisation's knowledge effectively . . . Both knowledge management and information literacy underpin the way the organisations work and develop. But such acceptance has not necessarily brought action.
3   Both are difficult concepts to 'sell' in terms of business values and outcomes. Both can be perceived as 'nice to have' or 'common sense' rather than a key organisational capability.

4    Both have had a problem with their label. Except for those in the know, the terms do not immediately conjure up a clear picture of what they mean.

(Abell and Skelton 2005)

Information literacy and knowledge management share problems of definition and recognition but they have complementary roles in the workplace and are complementary organisational ideologies. However they are most applicable in the larger organisation.

## Public libraries and information literacy

Since their foundation, public library services all over the world have played a role in informal and adult learning although it is often not a recognised one. In the UK the Public Libraries and Museums Act of 1964 placed upon local authorities a duty to provide 'a comprehensive and efficient service' although what a 'comprehensive and efficient service' actually means has never been defined. Although some services are mentioned they do not specifically include informal learning and information literacy skills training (Kelly 1977: 358–359). In an era of lifelong learning it can be suggested that this historic mission should be rediscovered, formalised and extended. As O'Beirne has argued: 'many would suggest that it is upon this informal learning, together with worthy principles of a liberal education for the masses, that the future of libraries will rest' (2010: 8).

Certainly the public library is in a strong position to promote information literacy skills development in the community (Harding 2008: 279). Strengths within the public library service include:

- The traditional and recognised role of the public library as a place of learning.
- From a community perspective librarians are considered to be information experts.
- The broad client base of public libraries is a strength when it comes to fostering the information literacy message.
- The public library often represents a child's first learning experience with formal information access, and from this perspective librarians are able to instil the importance and value of information and of the library as an information space.
- The public library has the ability to facilitate lifelong learning through their contact with members of the community who are interested in self-directed study or informal learning.
- The one-to-one relationship between public librarians and clients provides teachable moments (one-to-one reference training encounters).
- Public librarians have been effective in forming partnerships with other stakeholders (schools, government). This places them in a prime position to advocate the information literacy message.

- As key access points for the general public to information and ICT resources, the public library is in a strong position to provide training.

However, there are also weaknesses. Defining learner/stakeholder groups is difficult. A study of the information literacy environment in Canadian public libraries (Julien and Hoffman 2008) pointed out that:

- Training remained a comparatively minor priority with little formal training given.
- Clients are learning themselves and developing information literacy skills through experience and consulting with other people for advice and help rather than using formal training when offered by librarians.
- Funding dedicated to the task of information literacy was lacking.
- There was a lack of dedicated trained staff and space for training.

There is a lack of guidelines other than the general points made above and a lack of manuals of guidance or instruction. Perceptions of information literacy and information-literacy practice have tended to follow library-centric models blending bibliographic instruction with a user education model (Lloyd 2010: 133) and the pedagogy and skills needed for training in public libraries have received relatively little attention.

There is a grey area between informal and formal learning provision and it is difficult to draw a clear distinction between formal and informal learning. It is difficult to objectively measure successful training outcomes if no form of assessment is applied. It has been suggested that 'success' in a library situation depends on how learners feel about the learning experience regardless of whether they have completed a course or put their knowledge and skills to a particular purpose (McNicol and Dalton 2003). As O'Beirne puts it:

> By far the majority of learning that takes place in a public library is informal, often intangible, untainted by a credit framework and *ipso facto* personalised and relevant to the individual. It is also, by its nature, impossible to measure and thus difficult to dismiss or to defend.
>
> (2010: 12)

A study (Crawford and Irving 2012: 85–86) of an employability training course with a large information literacy element, run by Inverclyde Libraries in the west of Scotland, found that the most obvious benefit of the course was one which appeared, on the face of it, to be the most difficult to quantify: confidence. All the learners and the tutor, who based his conclusion on observing the students over the period of the course, were emphatic that their self-confidence had been greatly boosted by taking part in the course which is, in itself, an important factor in employability. What constitutes success may lead to a clash of cultures between libraries and other learning organisations.

There is also the issue of library staff roles and training. Staff may feel that they are not paid enough to take on teaching roles and the performance of such tasks may not appear in their job descriptions which might lead to disputes with relevant trade unions if they have no obligation to engage in teaching or training duties. Without proper training they may be unable to identify individual learners' needs. The issue of training/teaching styles needs to be addressed. The intellectually demanding, pedagogic higher education model is hardly suitable to people who have not progressed beyond secondary education and who may have found that experience negative and intimidating (Ashcroft et al 2007).

## Information policy definition and activity

Even a brief overview of these key areas shows the lack of certainty in information policy definition and activity although there is at least a role for information literacy within it and one which offers both opportunities and challenges to information literacy activity in non-formal and non-academic environments. This appears to take place in three connected stages. First, a nation perceives a need for competitive reasons to be a player in the global knowledge economy. Second, this suggests a need for the upskilling of its population to work effectively in this sort of economy, resulting in a national 'learning agenda'. The 'learning agenda' also tends to become explicitly associated with the skills of citizens, the development of these skills within educational programmes and their subsequent application in the workplace. Third, the growth of digital media and communications results in widespread information overload, leading to the need for both individuals and corporations to have effective information and knowledge management. This sequence tends to run from national concern to process analysis to products for developing information literacy (Town 2003: 86). In practice, process analysis and product development receive the most attention with most of the product development (learning and teaching materials) taking place in the education sector, primarily in higher education and much less in the lifelong learning and workplace sectors. Policy issues receive less attention.

What can be done to address this issue? While considerable progress has been made in moving information literacy from a 'library-centric' model to one which is more society and community based not enough has been done to integrate information-literacy policy making into public advocacy and indeed information-literacy policy making as a distinctive, systematic activity scarcely exists. ICT infrastructural and digital participation issues have achieved a much higher profile. It is difficult to see how much progress can be made without well-funded, centrally led strategies which can co-ordinate and support the many disparate initiatives which take place. There has been much debate as to whether information literacy activity should be a top-down activity or a bottom-up one in which it has hoped that numerous, local and disparate activities will somehow coalesce into a coherent whole. However well-intentioned the latter approach might be it has not achieved high profile results and Woody Horton, an expert in information literacy advocacy, champions the top-down approach (Horton 2011). A national agency of some sort, in all countries, is needed to develop initiatives and support those who are already making them at a regional or local level. The American National Forum on information literacy is a possible model for all but expert national organisations need to be staffed and funded although much can be achieved by a small number of people as the Welsh Information Literacy Project has shown (Welsh Information Literacy Project 2010). Such an agency might be led by the country's principal information organisation or at least have strong links with it. The primary motivation for setting up such an agency would almost certainly have to come from the country's principal information organisation as it is unlikely that any other body would have the expertise or will to do it.

What would such an agency do? Its first task would be to raise funding to support its activities and this must be an ongoing concern. Collaborative working with other bodies is essential and this applies to fund raising which should be sought in co-operation with universities and research bodies; charities including those concerned with deprivation issues; educational organisations and curriculum development agencies; relevant professional bodies; employers and employee organisations; chambers of commerce and skills and training agencies. It should have the support of the relevant government department which would probably be a ministry of education or lifelong learning. Collaborative working brings problems with it. Every organisation has its own distinctive aims and objectives and while these may overlap with information literacy they will not be the same and it is important to respect other's aims and objectives and show how information literacy can inform and support them. Its first and principal task should be the development of an information literacy policy in co-operation with the above bodies. Policy making must be realistic and should develop strands which will have appeal outside the information sector and are likely to attract funding. Particular attention should be paid to country's social and educational policies and policy and action should be mapped against them and topics should be included which appeal to government and the public. Internet safety and IPR issues are obvious examples. Policy making should recognise and work with innovative learning and teaching agendas which recognise independent learning and those who promote them as they are likely to be sympathetic to lifelong learning. An information literacy policy is, however, a process, not an event and it needs to be modified and developed as new needs emerge. As an Irish study points out the information literacy landscape is constantly changing (Connolly et al. 2013). For this reason documentation should be web based and evolving, rather than a fixed printed document. Advocacy and lobbying, carried out in partnership with other agencies, should draw on and enhance existing policies or as Woody Horton puts it: 'link information literacy to specific long standing goals and rewards' (Horton 2011: 273). It is important to bring together all information sectors to achieve a process of cross fertilisation so that the different sectors can learn from one another. Librarians working in higher education probably have the best developed skills in learning and teaching thanks to links with academic departments and educational development units and they are well placed to support other sectors. They could pass on their skills to other sectors. It is important that a national information literacy agency should support regional and local initiatives within the state by giving advice and guidance and acting as a link to relevant agencies and as a critical friend. It could well undertake evaluation work and one of its tasks might be to devise evaluation strategies. Cross-sectoral and collaborative working implies a community of practice. This might be web based, or consist of face-to-face meetings or, more probably, a combination of both. It should be a forum for the exchange of ideas and discussion of possible developments. Research projects relevant to the agency's policies should be undertaken, preferably in conjunction with relevant partners, both within and beyond the information sector. These will build up the agency's expertise and provide a base of knowledge to further develop policy and activity. The Scottish Information Literacy Project, for example, which ran from 2004 to 2010 was founded with the sole time-limited aim of developing an information literacy framework linking secondary and tertiary education but soon found, through a process of action research, that its remit needed to be widened to include the workplace, lifelong and informal learning (Irving 2011: 419–439).

Through collaboration with partners, exemplars of good practice and case studies should be collected and placed on the agency's website. These will both encourage and give status to those who have contributed them and will provide material which other partners can learn from, and use and develop themselves. It can also provide data to inform policy development and future action points.

Communication is important and the agency should write up and publish by whatever means are appropriate the results of its work. These might include a blog and other forms of social media, reporting at conferences and publication in appropriate journals. It should also organise conferences itself where its staff and partners can present; outside experts should also be invited to contribute. It should also develop evaluative criteria and undertake evaluation. As these are currently under developed this is an important function.

If a national information literacy programme is impossible then activity by a professional body is another possibility and this is probably the most favoured option. However, information literacy then has to take its place with a multiplicity of other information concerns. Time and resources are always constraints and information literacy has to compete with other priorities. A third and probably the cheapest option is to form a community of practice. Most of its work will probably be online but face to face meetings are also possible. An existing example is 'Information Skills for a 21st Century Scotland' (Scottish Library and Information Council 2012). It is an online community of practice which is open to everyone both within and outside the information profession, primarily in Scotland but also elsewhere. The community is open to everyone who is interested in information literacy and associated skills and competencies and wants to share practice, contribute to the community's knowledge of information literacy activities, and contribute case studies and news, reports of conferences and events and information about new research.

Formal education also has a role. Lifelong learning means just that but little work has been done on the earlier years in primary schools or nursery education and this is also an age group with whom librarians have little engagement. (Crawford and Irving 2013: 59–86). Information literacy skills can be taught at nursery and early years in primary schools. However it is difficult to make progress if teachers are not trained in information literacy skills and there is, as yet, little interest in information literacy in departments of education. Vigorous advocacy campaigns directed at departments of education and senior teachers are needed. It is also desirable that information literacy outcomes should be written into national school curricula. Links between school and public libraries are also important but it is important for teachers and librarians to co-operate, plan carefully and link activities to school curriculum outcomes. As with all information literacy activities we need to share, report at conferences and write about them more as sometimes great initiatives and projects go unnoticed. Information literacy is an information ideology with huge potential but also many challenges to face.

## References

Abell, A. and Skelton, V. (2005) Intellectual linking: making sense of the dots, *Library & Information Update*, 41 (1–2): 44–45.

American Library Association (1989) Presidential Committee on Information Literacy: final report. Chicago: ALA. Available at http://www.ala.org/ala/mgrps/divs/acrl/publications/whitepapers/presidential.cfm (accessed 19 November 2013).

Ashcroft, L., Farrow, J. and Watts, C. (2007) Public libraries and adult learners, *Library Management*, 28 (3): 125–138.

Australian Library and Information Association (2006) Statement on information literacy for all Australians. Available at http://www.alia.org.au/policies/information.literacy.html (accessed 19 November 2013).

Bawden, D. (2001) Information and digital literacies: a review of concepts, *Journal of Documentation*, 57 (2): 218–259.

Chartered Institute of Library and Information Professionals (2004) Information literacy definition. London: CILIP. Available at http://www.cilip.org.uk/get-involved/advocacy/learning/information-literacy/Pages/definition.aspx (accessed 19 November 2013).

Connolly, A., Curran, L., Lynch, A. and O'Shea, S. (2013) BILI: building information literacy in Ireland, *Library and Information Research*, 37(114): 37–54.

Cooke, L. and Greenwood, H. (2008) 'Cleaners don't need computers': bridging the digital divide in the workplace. *ASLIB Proceedings*, 60(2): 143–157.

Crawford, J. and Irving, C. (2009) Information literacy in the workplace: a qualitative exploratory study, *Journal of Librarianship and Information Science* (41) 1, 29–38. Available at http://lis.sagepub.com/cgi/content/abstract/41/1/29?etoc (accessed 19 November 2013).

Crawford, J. and Irving, C. ( 2012) Information literacy in employability training: the experience of Inverclyde Libraries, *Journal of Librarianship and Information Science*, 44(2): 79–89.

Crawford, J. and Irving, C. (2013) *Information literacy and lifelong learning: policy issues, the workplace, health and public libraries*. Oxford: Chandos.

Doyle, C. S. (1994) *Information literacy in an information society: a concept for the information age*. Syracuse, NY: ERIC Clearinghouse. (ED 372763).

Ferguson, S (2009) Information literacy and its relationship to knowledge management. *Journal of Information Literacy*, 3(2): 6–24. Available at http://ojs.lboro.ac.uk/ojs/index. php/JIL/article/viewArticle/PRA-V3-I2-2009-1 (accessed 19 November 2013).

Garner, S. D. (2005) High-level colloquium on information literacy and lifelong learn- ing. Available from: http://www.ifla.org/publications/high-level-colloquium-on- information-literacy-and-lifelong-learning (accessed 19 November 2013).

Harding, J. N. (2008) Information literacy and the public library: we've talked the talk but are we walking the walk? *Australian Library Journal*, 56: 48–62.

Horton, F. W. (2008) *Understanding information literacy: a primer*. Paris: UNESCO.

Horton, F. W. (2011) Information literacy advocacy: Woody's ten commandments, *Library Trends*, 60(2): 262–276.

Irving, C. (2011) National information literacy framework (Scotland): pioneering work to influence policy making or tinkering at the edges, *Library Trends*, 60(2): 419–439

Julien, H. and Hoffman, C. (2008) Information literacy training in Canada's public libraries, *Library Quarterly* 78(1): 19–41.

Kelly, T. (1977) *A history of public libraries in Great Britain, 1845–1975*. London: Library Association.

Lloyd, A. (2009) Informing practice: information experiences of ambulance officers in train- ing and on-road practice. *Journal of Documentation*, 65(3): 396–419.

Lloyd, A. (2010) *Information literacy landscapes*. Oxford: Chandos.

Lloyd, A. (2011) Trapped between a rock and a hard place: what counts as informa- tion literacy in the workplace and how is it conceptualized? *Library Trends*, 60(2): 277–296.

McNicol, S. and Dalton, P. (2003) Public libraries: supporting the learning process. Centre for Information Research, University of Central England, Birmingham. Available at http://www.ebase.bcu.ac.uk/cirtarchive/projects/past/public_libraries.htm (accessed 20 November 2012).

O'Beirne, R. (2010) *From lending to learning: the development and extension of public libraries*. Oxford: Chandos.

Pinto, M., Cordon, J. A and Diaz, R. G. (2010) Thirty years of information literacy (1977– 2007): a terminological, conceptual and statistical analysis, *Journal of Librarianship and Information Science*, 42(1): 3–19.

Scottish Library and Information Council (2012) Information skills for a 21st century Scotland. Available at http://www.therightinformation.org/ (accessed 21 November 2013).

Society of College, National and University Libraries (2011). The SCONUL Seven Pillars of Information Literacy, core model for higher education. Available at https://www. sconul.ac.uk/groups/information_literacy/publications/coremodel.pdf (accessed 20 November 2013).

Town, J. S. (2003) Information literacy and the information society. In Hornby, S. and Clark, Z. (eds) *Challenge and change in the information society*. London: Facet.

UNESCO (2003) The Prague Declaration: towards an information literate society. Prague: UNESCO. Available at: http://portal.unesco.org/ci/en/files/19636/11228863531Prag ueDeclaration.pdf/PragueDeclaration.pdf (accessed 21 November 2013).

UNESCO (2009) *National information society policy: a template.* Paris: UNESCO.

Weiner, S. (2011). Information literacy and the workforce: a review, *education libraries*, (34) 2, 7–14. Available at http://units.sla.org/division/ded/educationlibraries/34-2.pdf (accessed 20 November 2013).

Welsh Information Literacy Project (2010) Current practice in Wales. [Cardiff]: Welsh Information Literacy Project. Available at: http://library.wales.org/en/information-literacy/case-studies/ (accessed 20 November 2013).

Wikipedia (2010) Knowledge management. Available at http://en.wikipedia.org/wiki/ Knowledge_management (accessed 20 November 2013).

Zurkowski, P. (1974) *The information environment: relationships and priorities.* Washington, DC. National Commission on Libraries and Information Science.

# Chapter 8

# Moving with the times
## How mobile digital literacies are changing childhood

*Guy Merchant*

## Introduction

Not so long ago we thought of a computer as a thing to go to, housed in a purpose-built laboratory or chained to a desk. Its users were assumed to be highly-skilled adults – specialists operating on the frontiers of knowledge. Nowadays many of us carry around more computing power in our pockets and use smartphones, on a daily basis, to co-ordinate our activities and to stay in touch with family and friends. In some ways we are all specialists now, and the rapid take-up of mobile devices has prompted us to develop new practices as we have adjusted our relationships and connections with one another, and developed new ways of meaning-making. As a result literacies are changing; not because of technology but because of the ways in which it is put to use in everyday life.

Recognition of these changes and their impact on how we think about literacy and communication as social practices has been outlined in a number of influential texts that have emerged since the turn of the century (such as Cope & Kalantzis, 2000; Kress, 2003 and Lankshear & Knobel, 2010). They describe, albeit in their different ways, changes in the communicative context and suggest that literacies are increasingly multiple, multimodal and mediated through new technology.

For those working in the field of literacy education, an acknowledgement of this new communicative context has raised many complex questions. Among them has been a concern for how a curriculum might reflect new uses of literacy, and how schools and other institutions might best prepare the young for a rapidly evolving digital future. And, in a complementary endeavour, researchers have also become interested in students' varied experiences of digital culture, what it is they already have access to and experience of – what some commentators have described as their 'digital capital'.

Until relatively recently this body of work has focused on older children and teenagers. The early years, and the early stages of literacy learning, have attracted far less attention. Burnett (2010) illustrates this in her review of empirical studies of technology and literacy in educational settings. She found only 36 papers published between 2003 and 2009 that were focused on the 0–8 age range. Nevertheless work documented by Marsh (2005), Plowman & McPake (2010), Wohlwend (2013) and others has helped to set a research agenda that focuses on the way in which the literacies of new technologies are taken up by young children.

On the basis of this emerging body of evidence, we can fairly confidently assume that most young children, particularly those growing up in affluent economic contexts, are immersed in a densely mediated communicative environment from the very beginning. Take, for example, the fact that the first images of a baby are usually scans displayed on computer screens and mobile phones (Burnett & Merchant, 2012), and how pictures of new-born babies are routinely shared on handheld devices, distributed to family and friends via instant messaging and then published on social networking sites. From this point of view, babies are born digital, immersed in an environment which is already patterned with the traces of communication technologies.

From the outset, we know that most babies will spend quite a bit of time looking at screens (Rideout & Hammel, 2006), they may well be shown a mobile phone to distract or comfort them (Oksman & Rautiainen, 2003) and in many cases their first toys will come with digital components. An increasingly wide range of games and activity centres designed for young babies now have digital components, and so do baby walkers, play mats and plush toys. Products aimed at young children, such as those developed by highly successful specialist companies such as *Callaway Digital Arts* and *vTech,* discussed below, characterise this new development. Embedded in these toys are digitally reproduced nursery rhymes, counting games and alphabet songs providing 'edutainment' for infants and toddlers (Burnett & Merchant, 2012). Furthermore these products are often connected to transmedia narratives depicting characters from film and television – narratives that 'flow across different forms and platforms' (Jenkins et al., 2006:86).

Not only then are babies and toddlers immersed in an environment in which digital communication is common place through the everyday lives of their parents, carers, siblings and so on, but also there is a gradual infusion of the digital into the activities and playthings that they encounter, interact with and explore. These playthings are what Dyson (1996) describes as 'textual toys' and are embedded in a wider media culture. Pursuing this theme, what follows is an exploration of the changing landscape of early digital literacies in childhood – an exploration that is informed by perspectives from literacy studies with its emphasis on situated practice (Barton & Lee, 2013; Scollon & Scollon, 2004); through the concept of 'sociomateriality' which sees the social and the material as mutually constitutive (Suchman, 2002); and through analyses of the political economy of edutainment (Buckingham & Scanlon, 2005).

The chapter begins by exploring the role of digital playthings in early literacy with reference to discourses of parenting and the emergence of parental pedagogies. I then use two contrasting examples to illustrate how popular play objects may contribute to the digital ecology of early childhood. Here I am concerned with what such a focus can tell us about the messages and meaning-making potential that are designed into digital toys and games, through a conceptualisation of them as textual toys. However, in doing this I am not advocating an exclusive focus on play objects in isolation, and acknowledge that such objects only take on meaning when read and used in social contexts, but suggest, nonetheless, that there is something to be gained through looking at their distribution and materiality, and the discourses in which they are embedded.

## Digital playthings and early literacy

Toys and toy manufacturers have always played an important part in early childhood. Their role in young children's learning is arguably ill-defined and certainly under-explored and under-theorised – notwithstanding semiotic studies of play objects such as those by Briggs (2007); Machin and Van Leeuwen (2009) and Pennel (1994). This is especially true for early literacy development in which everything from alphabet building blocks and jigsaw puzzles to the best-selling educational tablet, the *LeapPad* (Leapfrog, 2013), carries implicit messages about what literacy is, how it develops and what roles adults, care-givers and children should adopt. What is more, these implied roles blend in with current conceptions of parenting, and are themselves unavoidably bound up with wider social, cultural, political and economic forces. Witness the recent emergence of a new governmentality of parenting through 'social investment' initiatives (Jensen & Saint-Martin, 2006); initiatives that reach into the every-day relationships between children and adults to underscore the significance of both what is *done with* as well as what is *provided for* the very young. This, I argue has helped to shape the political economy of educational playthings.

As Nichols et al. observe, neo-liberal policies that address early childhood education repeatedly emphasise the important formative role that parents and carers play in early literacy learning. Policies, projects and interventions – both nationally and locally – often give explicit attention to early language and literacy, and they work alongside 'commercially sponsored services and products' in contributing to the discursive construction of the 'good parent' (2009: 65). Furthermore, this newly conceived emphasis on a particular kind of parenting puts adult care-givers under increasing pressure to invest in early learning as young children's progress becomes competitively marked by various baseline assessments. Pre-school edutainment has thus become a burgeoning new market in which commercial interests vie for the attention of parents who are encouraged to buy early educational advantage (Buckingham & Scanlon, 2005).

Publishers and toy manufacturers have been quick to see the lucrative potential, and as they explore how digital technology might enhance their products, their marketing and their distribution, a new generation of digital playthings has emerged. As we have seen, digital rhymes, counting games and alphabet songs are ubiquitous in the lives of many babies and toddlers. And these toys themselves are certainly not passive objects – not only are they carefully scripted, but they are often programmed to 'wake-up' after a period of inactivity, to begin an audio-visual action sequence prompted by gentle touch, movement or accidental collision in the toy box. A clearer example of what Latour (2005) describes as 'non-human actants' would indeed be hard to find, and it could be argued that in some respects adult or parental activity has been 'delegated' to these technological toys.

In investigating the materiality of these playthings, the concept of affordances is useful in helping us to read the material and semiotic potential that they present. This much contested concept (see Norman, 1999) gives us some purchase on the relationship between the plaything-as-object and the ways in which humans (in this case young children) might interact, or relate to it. In this analysis affordances are seen as: 'potentials for action that depend on both the material properties of objects and the ability of actors to perceive and use them' (Robey at al., 2012: 224).

In what follows I examine how these affordances involve digital technology in acts of literacy instruction that are generated through, and by, interaction with toys and games. At the same time I set this in the context of the discursive construction of early literacy through examining the marketing and business priorities of the producers. The initial focus is on two distinct playthings, both very popular with global distribution: the *First Steps Baby Walker* (vTech) and the *Endless Alphabet* (Callaway Digital Arts). Analysis of these products is used to exemplify the increasing commodification of early learning and the ways in which digital technology, combined with dominant discourses about parenting, is reshaping early literacy.

### The First Steps Baby Walker

vTech is a Hong Kong-based manufacturer of electronic goods with worldwide distribution. Founded in 1976, it specialises in portable electronic goods and its core business is manufacturing and distributing cordless phones and electronic learning products (ELPs). On its corporate website, vTech claims to be the number one supplier of ELPs in the US and Western Europe, with a distribution network covering 84 countries worldwide and a strategy to increase its presence in China, Australia and Japan (www.vtech.com). The company's focus on learning is quite explicit, claiming on its promotional website that: 'When it comes to education, you can't beat something that makes it fun'.

ELPs developed by vTech are, of course, marketed directly to parents. So, for example, the baby section of vtechuk.com carries the strap line 'We put more into our toys . . . so your child gets more out of them' and is accompanied by carousel images of smiling babies from different ethnic backgrounds holding and grasping brightly coloured plastic toys. Below this it displays the following message:

> The VTech Baby range has been designed to bring out the best in babies, infants and toddlers by encouraging them to **play, learn and discover**. It stimulates the senses and imagination by introducing **shapes, colours, objects, numbers and letters**, which help to develop a child's mental and physical abilities.
>
> (vTech UK, 2013)

This sets out an explicitly educational and developmental view of the early years – one in which exploring the environment (and by implication vTech toy products) is about play, learning and discovery with an emphasis on content that might be more commonly associated with an early years, nursery or kindergarten curriculum. These acts of exploration are to be guided by the good parent who plays a key role 'in influencing a child's cognitive, language, motor and social-emotional development' (ibid). Further tips are provided by vTech, which include an elaboration on language development for parents:

> Engage your baby in **face-to-face interaction** so they can:
>
> * Hear language being spoken
> * Listen to the written word read aloud
> * Practice associating objects with words
>
> (vTech UK, 2013)

Although these are relatively simple pieces of advice for parents, they carry the hallmarks of those familiar lists of performative statements that have come to characterise curriculum documents both in their grammatical structure and layout (cf. DfE, 2013).

Available in two versions, one in primary colours and the other in pink tones, catering presumably for parental preference related to gender, the *First Steps Baby Walker* is part of this baby range. Figure 8.1 is an annotated image from the *vTech* website that shows one of the models and draws attention to the toy's affordances. In essence the baby walker responds to different kinds of physical interactions that include pressing, pulling and turning. Although a number of these affordances have relevance to language and literacy development, some of are more overt than others. Two of these stand out. Firstly, the 'wake up' sequence, that plays as soon as batteries are inserted, or when the baby walker is moved or nudged – as soon, that is, that an adult or child makes direct physical contact with it:

> Wuff! Wuff! Wuff!
> Hello baby. [spoken]
> Hello puppy calling, do you want to play with me?
> Let's have fun together as you learn your ABC!
> [sung to musical accompaniment]

This serves to highlight one of the pedagogical functions of this electronic learning product – the literacy component of the baby walker. Secondly, there is the keyboard. Located on the lower part of the toy and made out of brightly-coloured, semi-transparent plastic, this comprises five keys inscribed with the letters a–e each accompanied by an appropriate picture (apple, ball, car etc.). When activated, lights play in a random sequence behind these transparent keys to attract the child's attention. Pressing the 'a' key generates a spoken voice that will say 'a is for apple' followed by the sound of an apple being bitten into. Similar information is given on pressing each one of the letter keys. Letter identification uses the phonic pronunciation of the letter's 'sound'.

From the initial injunction to have fun and to learn the letters of the alphabet and into the formulaic introduction to the letters themselves presented on the keyboard, highlights alphabetic literacy. It could be said that what it offers is a parody of literacy instruction, in which letter sounds (phonics) are connected with simple illustrations. This is a model of literacy learning that is traditional, skill-based and suggestive of rote learning, based upon the first five letters of the alphabet. For all the technology that sits behind the *First Steps Baby Walker* this is very much old-school literacy.

The material affordances of the baby walker are where the design is arguably more carefully matched to the needs of the target age-group. In its overall shape and height, the toy provides support for standing upright, whereas the proportions and placing of the wheels aid forward motion – the so-called

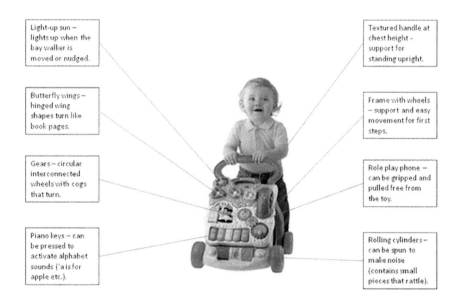

*Figure 8.1* The affordances of the vTech *First Steps Baby Walker*

first steps. As illustrated in the annotations in Figure 8.1, the various smaller features both invite and reward tactile exploration, particularly the fine-motor movements of gripping, spinning, turning and pressing. But despite vTech's best efforts to tie their products to early alphabetic literacy, this toy does relatively little to support that, but yet at the same time it undoubtedly promotes the message that what counts in early literacy development is de-contextualized letter recognition, and in doing this it contributes to the peda-gogic discourses that are beginning to 'curricularize' adult–child interactions in the home (Briggs, 2009).

### The Endless Alphabet

vTech's baby walker could in some respects be seen as a familiar sort of toy, the natural successor to the push-and-pull brick trolley, a play object that sup-ports the transition from crawling to walking, and one that provides added opportunities for play and learning. It is not so easy to trace the provenance of the second sort of play object under analysis. *Endless Alphabet* is a letter play app designed for the iPad, iPhone and iPod Touch, available for download at the Apple App Store.

Once started, the app shows a screen with a central display of a single word which is surrounded by colourful letters that comprise that word. The task is to match the letters to the word (see Figure 8.2). On successful completion a short animation is generated and this illustrates the word's meaning. The child is then free to scroll through a bank of unrelated words to choose another. If there are any similarities between the *Endless Alphabet* and pre-digital forms, the closest fit would be the letter-matching board game.

*Endless Alphabet* is produced by New York-based Callaway Digital Arts, a subsidiary of Callaway Arts and Entertainment, founded in 2010. Like vTech, Callaway Digital Arts pitches explicitly to the parent-as-educator, aiming to publish: 'the most entertaining and educational mobile apps for kids and fami-lies [ . . . .] digital experiences beloved and respected by kids, parents, and edu-cators' (Callaway Digital Arts, 2013a).

Interviewed in 2012, founder Nicholas Callaway describes how he: ' . . . foresaw the era in which the primary medium for entertainment and learning would be mobile and tablet devices' (Greenfield, 2012). In this vision, resources for the good parent are app-based games and texts that are down-loaded to their portable devices, available anywhere and anytime. In Callaway Digital Arts, literacy is a key focus and marketing material emphasises the importance of early success in reading through letter recognition, vocabulary building – and fun:

> Set the stage for reading success with this delightfully interactive edu-cational app. Kids will have a blast learning their ABC's and building vocabulary with the adorable monsters in Endless Alphabet. Each word

features an interactive puzzle game with talking letters and a short animation illustrating the definition.

(Callaway Digital Arts, 2013b)

So, much like vTech, the producers of *Endless Alphabet* are contributing to the
construction of an early literacy curriculum for young children through a direct
connection with parents. But in this case the product is curiously immaterial
(Burnett, 2011), with data and software stored as bitstrings (Yoo, 2012:139)
accessible only through the touchscreen affordances of the mobile device. To
play *Endless Alphabet*, the child (or adult) touches one of the coloured letters
on the screen and in a 'drag-and-drop' move matches it up with the outline in
the centre of the screen (see Figure 8.2). This requires some precision in fine
motor control – contact with the screen must be maintained throughout this
operation.

When initial contact is made with a coloured letter, it animates by increasing in size, dancing around a little and adopting an animal-like form with the
addition of an eye, mouth or nose.

Touching a coloured letter also activates the repeated phonic sound of the
letter, which continues until it reaches the correct destination (Figure 8.3). At
that point it can be released and allowed to settle into place as the sound of the
letter name plays. A wrong match is greeted with an 'er-her' or similar noise
to indicate negative feedback. Successful completion of the matching exercise
prompts the app to generate a recorded human voice that clearly enunciates the
whole word. This is followed by cheers and applause, a short animation and

*Figure 8.2* Screenshot of *Endless Alphabet*

*Figure 8.3  Endless Alphabet – working at the interface*

a spoken definition. In the example shown in Figure 8.1 this runs as follows: 'When you dye something you are changing its colour. Usually you dye hair or fabric'.

The material affordances of *Endless Alphabet* are inseparable from those of the touchscreen itself. In other words, interaction with the game involves what has been described as the effortless performance of human touch (Robles-de-la-Torre, 2006: 24). As can be seen in Figure 8.3, the young child simply operates at the interface to touch, drag and drop the letters into place whilst the app presents the options, provides feedback and finally rewards successful completion by playing the short animation. Like the *First Steps Baby Walker* the app delivers the familiar literacy routine of letter recognition and matching. Although there is a more sophisticated design at work, the literacy involved is essentially that of encoding and decoding.

By using updates and reminders Callaway Digital Arts also exploits a key feature of mobile technology. The alphabet is, in a manner of speaking, endless as new vocabulary is pushed to the user on a regular basis, and this flow of content is signalled by alerts on the icon when the mobile device is activated. In its appearance then, as app-based edutainment available for different devices using touchscreen technology, the *Endless Alphabet* relies on everyday digital literacies and it depends on this for both delivery and activation; but at the same time it reinforces the idea of literacy instruction as skill development, playing into the ways in which the good parent prepares the child for reading success.

## Digital literacy and the commodification of early learning

The *First Steps Baby Walker* and the *Endless Alphabet* represent two quite different ways in which small-scale electronic and digital technology takes shape in the lives of babies and toddlers. They illustrate distinctive ways in which the mobile and the digital have become enmeshed with early play and exploration – activities that are infused with ideologies about early learning and the development of literacy. Although the commodification of early learning is not a new phenomenon, the ways in which toy manufacturers are appropriating the discourse of the good parent represents a strengthening of their reach and influence, particularly with respect to digital literacy.

Analysing the marketing, production and distribution of digital playthings reveals some important issues and contradictions in contemporary thinking about early literacy. First, despite the ubiquitous presence of digital literacy in the everyday lives of young children, it seems that many of the toys and games that they will encounter are designed to deliver a skills-based view of literacy – learning that focuses on vocabulary, letter recognition and spelling. Despite the fact that these toys and games may contain digital components, or use the internet for delivery and updating, their primary purpose is considerably less adventurous. If we acknowledge that from a social-practice perspective what counts as literacy and consequently who counts as literate is inseparable from context, the two games and toys that have been considered, and countless others like them, construct early literacy as the performance of simple de-contextualized skills. Yet at the same time, babies and young children are immersed more widely in a densely mediated communicative environment, apprenticed to newer and more complex acts of meaning-making. In this respect Wohlwend (2009) is quite right to argue that these home practices cannot simply be put aside as children enter the more formal institutions of early childhood education, and to call for the recognition of digital literacy in the early stages of schooling. But there is also another task for literacy educators, and that is to help parents, policy makers and producers to negotiate some rather complex debates about early literacy and to understand how so-called simple models reduce and restrict literacy, and produce models of parental pedagogy that promote early indicators of success through the performance of traditional skills.

Second, in a related move, toy manufacturers in their design choices and in their marketing materials, contribute to the discursive construction of the good parent as one who invests in playthings that are 'educational' and supports the development of these self-same basic skills. This plays into what I described earlier as the new governmentality of parenting which works in conjunction with services and products creating a political economy located in the global mediascape (Appadurai, 1996). In these discourses, the early years become 'cur-ricularized' and are seen simply as a stage of preparation for future activity – the real business of schooling. An example of this is the way in which the UK gov-ernment has branded birth to five as the 'Foundation Stage', informing parents that this is an important time for helping children 'get ready for school' and 'preparing them for future learning and success' (EYFS, 2012: 1). This shifts the emphasis from immediate needs and preoccupations as the present of the early years is mortgaged to the future schooling of citizens-in-the-making.

Third, there is the crucial issue of how all these factors enter into specific, localised and moment-to-moment actions and interactions in homes and early years settings. Whilst this chapter has focused exclusively on toys and games themselves, this is an incomplete picture. An account is needed of how these discourses (and others) are instantiated in everyday experiences along with individual histories, ideas and attitudes and indeed the whole spectrum of situ-ational influences. Here the idea of a nexus analysis is a useful way of articu-lating this complexity (Scollon & Scollon, 2004). This perspective can help to capture play practices that are singular and situated, whilst at the same time acknowledging how the play objects themselves are part of a political economy located in a global mediascape.

Figure 8.4 uses the nexus concept to illustrate the confluence of these themes in moment-to-moment instances of play. Babies' and toddlers' exploration of digital playthings is conceived of as social action in which discourses, including those referred to above, and the sort of sociomaterial interactions I have described work together to pattern the singularity of that moment. This suggests a future direction for work in early years literacy research in which the idea of the 'nexus of practice' (Scollon & Scollon, 2004) can be taken up to critique the practices of early literacy and the place of the digital in different contexts. Pioneering work by Wohlwend and Buchholz (2014) shows how this line of inquiry might take shape.

## Conclusion

Considering the ubiquity of digital literacies in the everyday lives of young chil-dren it is surprising how little empirical work has focused on new literacies and play in the early years. The dominance of developmental models that empha-sise what is 'natural' or 'age-appropriate' have relatively easily combined with discourses that encourage a return to the basic skills of literacy with the effect

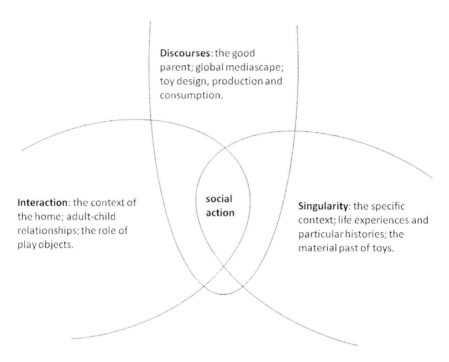

Discourses: the good
parent; global mediascape;
toy design, production and
consumption.

Interaction: the context of
the home; adult-child
relationships; the role of
play objects.

social
action

Singularity: the specific
context; life experiences and
particular histories; the
material past of toys.

*Figure 8.4* A nexus analysis of textual toys
Source: Adapted from Scollon and Scollon (2004)

that digital literacy is repeatedly pressed into service to deliver the rote learning of alphabetic skills. The limited focus of existing research is also linked to the predominance of cognitive models of reading which have tended to position technology as a tool for skill development as opposed to a medium for diverse social practices (Hassett, 2006). Research that focuses on 'being' rather than 'becoming' literate (see Burnett & Merchant, 2013; Leander & Boldt, 2013) begins to draw our attention to the place of new technology in the ecology of meaning-making – the broader context of children's early learning. In this sense the current chapter contributes to understanding about digital literacies in early childhood by illustrating how a focus on digital playthings and their place in a nexus of discourses helps to structure how we see early literacy development.

## References

Appadurai, A. (1996) *Modernity at Large: Cultural Dimensions of Globalization*. Minneapolis: Minnesota University Press.
Barton, D. & Lee, C. (2013). *Language Online: Investigating Digital Texts and Practices*. London: Routledge.
Briggs, M. (2007). 'Teddy Bears, Television and Play: Rethinking Semiosis in Children's Media Culture.' *Social Semiotics* 17(4): 503–524.

Briggs, M. (2009) 'BBC Children's Television, Parentcraft and Pedagogy: Towards the Ethicalization of Existence.' *Media, Culture & Society* 31(1): 32–29.

Buckingham, D. & Scanlon, M. (2001) 'Parental Pedagogies: An Analysis of British Edutainment Magazines for Young Children.' *Journal of Early Childhood Literacy* 1(3): 281–299.

Buckingham, D. & Scanlon, M. (2005) 'Selling Learning: Towards a Political Economy of Edutainment Media.' *Media, Culture & Society* 27(1): 41–58.

Burnett, C. (2010). 'Technology and Literacy in Early Childhood Educational Settings: A Review of Research.' *Journal of Early Childhood Literacy*, 10(3): 247–270.

Burnett, C. (2011). 'The (im)materiality of educational space: Interactions between material, connected and textual dimensions of networked technology use in schools.' E-*Learning and Digital Media*, 8(2): 14–227.

Burnett, C. & Merchant, G. (2012). 'Learning, literacies and new technologies: the current context and future possibilities.' In J. Larson & J. Marsh (eds), *The Handbook of Early Literacy*. London: Sage.

Burnett, C. & Merchant, G. (2013). 'Points of view: reconceptualising literacies through an exploration of adult and child interactions in a virtual world.' *Journal of Research in Reading*. DOI:10.1111/jrir.12006.

Callaway Digital Arts (2013a) 'About us.' Accessed 12th November 2013 at: http://originatorkids.com/about/

Callaway Digital Arts (2013b) 'Endless Alphabet.' Accessed 12th November 2013 at: http://originatorkids.com/category/apps/

Cope, B. & Kalantzis, M. (2000). *Multiliteracies: Literacy Learning and the Design of Social Futures*. London: Routledge.

DfE (2013) Statutory *Framework for the Early Years Foundation Stage*. Runcorn: Department for Education.

EYFS (2012) 'Parents Guide to the Early Years Foundation Stage Framework. Department for Education.' Accessed 12th November 2013 at http://www.foundationyears.org.uk

Dyson, A.H. (1996) 'Cultural Constellations and Childhood: On Greek Gods, Cartoon Heroes, and the Social Lives of Schoolchildren.' *Harvard Educational Review* 6(3): 471–495.

Greenfield, J. (2012). 'Callaway Digital Arts Founder Nicholas Callaway on Building the Publishing Company of the Future.' Digital Book World March 13th, 2012. Accessed 12th November 2013 at: http://www.digitalbookworld.com/2012/callaway-digital-arts-founder-nicholas-callaway-on-building-the-publishing-company-of-the-future/

Greenhow, C. & Robelia, B. (2009) 'Informal Learning and Identity Formation in Online Social Networks.' *Learning, Media and Technology*, 34(2): 119–140.

Hassett, D. (2006) 'Signs of the Times: The Governance of Alphabetic Print over "Appropriate" and "Natural" Reading Development.' *Journal of Early Childhood Literacy*, 6(1): 77–103.

Jenkins, H., Purushota, R., Clinton, K., Weigel, M. & Robinson, A. (2006) Confronting the Challenges of Participatory Culture: Media Education for the 21st Century Chicago: MacArthur Foundation. Accessed 12th November 2013 at: http://digitallearning.macfound.org/

Jenson, J. & Saint-Martin, D. (2006) 'Building Blocks for a New Social Architecture: The LEGO (TM) Paradigm of an Active Society.' *Policy and Politics* 34(3): 429–451.

Kress, G. (2003). *Literacy in the New Media Age*. London: Routledge.

Lankshear, C. & Knobel, M. (2010) *New Literacies: Everyday Practices and Social Learning* (3rd Edition). Maidenhead: Open University Press.

Latour, B. (2005) *Reassembling the Social: An Introduction to Actor-Network Theory*. Oxford: Oxford University Press.

Leander, K. & Boldt, G. (2013) 'Rereading "A Pedagogy of Multiteracies": Bodies, Texts, and Emergence.' *Journal of Literacy Research* 45(1): 22–46.

Leapfrog (2013) 'LeapPad.' Accessed 12th November 2013 at: http://www.leapfrog.com/en_gb/landingpages/leappadultra.html

Machin, D. & Van Leeuwen, T. (2009) 'Toys as discourse: Children's War Toys and the War On Terror.' *Critical Discourse Studies*, 6(1): 51–63.

Marsh, J. (ed.) (2005) *Popular Culture, New Media and Digital Literacy in Early Childhood.* London: Routledge.

Nichols, S., Nixon, H. & Rowsell, J. (2009). 'The 'Good' Parent in Relation to Early Childhood Literacy: Symbolic Terrain and Lived Practice.' *Literacy* 43(2): 65–75.

Nixon, H. & Hateley, E. (2013) 'Books, Toys and Tablets: Playing and Learning in the Age of Digital Media.' In K. Hall, T. Cremin, B. Comber & L. Moll (eds.) *International Handbook of Research on Children's Literacy, Learning, and Culture.* Oxford: Wiley-Blackwell, pp. 28–41.

Norman, D. (1999) 'Affordances, Conventions and Design.' *Interactions* 6(3): 38–42.

Oksman, V. & Rautiainen, P. (2003) '"Perhaps it Is a Body Part": How the Mobile Phone Became an Organic Part of the Everyday Lives of Finnish Children and Teenagers' in J.E. Katz (ed) *Machines that Become Us: the Social Context of Personal Communication Technology.* New Jersey: Transaction, pp. 293–311.

Pennell, G. E. (1994) 'Babes in Toyland: Learning an Ideology of Gender.' *Advances in Consumer Research* 21(1): 359–364.

Plowman, L. & McPake, S. (2010) *Growing Up With Technology: Young Children Learning in a Digital World.* London: Routledge.

Rideout, V. J. & Hammel, E. (2006) *The Media Family: Electronic Media in the Lives of Infants, Toddlers, Preschoolers and their Parents.* Menlo Park, CA: Kaiser Family Foundation.

Robey, D., Raymond, B. & Anderson, C. (2012) 'Theorizing Information Technology as a Material Artifact.' In P. Leonardi, B. Nardi, & J. Kallinikos (eds) *Materiality and Organizing: Social Interaction in a Technological World.* Oxford: Oxford University Press, pp. 217–236.

Robles-de-la-Torre, G.(2006) 'The Importance of the Sense of Touch in Virtual and Real Environments,' *IEEE Multimedia* 13(3): 24–30.

Scollon, R. & Scollon, S. W. (2004) *Nexus Analysis: Discourse and the Emerging Internet.* New York: Routledge.

Suchman, L. (2002) 'Located Accountabilities in Technology Production.' *Scandinavian Journal of Information Systems* 14(2): 91–105.

vTech UK (2013) 'vTech Baby.' Accessed 12th November 2013 at: http://www.vtechuk.com/vtech-baby/

Wohlwend, K. (2009) 'Early Adopters: Playing New Literacies and Pretending New Technologies in Print-Centric Classrooms.' *Journal of Early Childhood Literacy* 9(2): 117–140.

Wohlwend, K. (2013) *Literacy Playshop: Playing with the New Literacies and Popular Media in the Early Childhood Classroom.* New York: Teachers College Press.

Wohlwend, K., & Buchholz, B. (2014) 'Paper Pterodactyls and Popsicle Sticks: Expanding School Literacy through Film-making and Toy-making.' In C. Burnett, J. Davies, G. Merchant & J. Rowsell (eds) *New Literacies around the Globe: Policy and Pedagogy.* London: Routledge.

Yoo, Y. (2012) 'Digital Materiality and the Emergence of an Evolutionary Science of the Artificial.' In P. Leonardi, B. Nardi, & J. Kallinikos (eds) *Materiality and Organizing: Social Interaction in a Technological World.* Oxford: Oxford University Press, pp. 134–154.

# Chapter 9

# Afterword

## Locating adult literacy education in new places

*David Barton*

## Introduction

This chapter will draw conclusions on the ways in which we must respond to the demands of the twenty-first century, how we must position literacy through specific curricula in order to make it acceptable to funders and to enable it to meet the impending and emergent challenges. Drawing on the previous chapters the key theme will be 'what's next?'.

The word 'literacy' can have many meanings and what is meant by the term is influenced by the words around it. Within this book we can see many meanings as 'literacy' is juxtaposed with several other terms. The book starts out from a basic question which has been at the heart of Literacy Studies for more than 20 years: *What is literacy?* The question can be constantly re-asked in the chapters of the book. At the same time the chapters go forwards by locating discussions around literacy in contemporary issues and by linking in with other areas.

## Discussion

Right from the beginning of the book, the editors make it clear that they are concerned with 'adult literacy', a term which implicitly has the word 'education' in there: 'adult literacy' usually means 'adult literacy education', and education is the focus of the contributions to this book. The editors then place a framework of the three Ps – policy, perceptions and practice – over the term as a triangle, so that there can be discussions along each of the three sides of the triangle, investigating the links between policy and practice; between perceptions and practice; and between perceptions and policy. This is the focus of the first chapter.

Of course, the three Ps are not straightforward in meaning. 'Policy' can be a set of detailed centrally imposed rules of what governments want to happen, or the term can be used to mean locally agreed conventions to guide practice. 'Practice' itself can simply mean what is generally done, and this can refer to everyday practice or it can refer to educational practice. When used in the plural, as 'practices', the meaning gets close to the use of the third word, 'perception'. Here this is used in the book to refer to the sense people make of literacy and how this guides their actions, that is their theories of literacy.

The point of the book is to show how these terms have changed in meaning over time and, more importantly, how the relations between them have also changed – so, for instance, how policy has changed in importance as an influence over educational practice, and how theories have risen and fallen as influences on educational practice. As an example of this, in the 1970s in England there was no central government policy on adult literacy education. There were local initiatives and locally based projects to support adults with problems reading and writing. These were often provided and supported through community groups and included a strong student writing movement. At the time there was a concerted movement, the Right to Read campaign, calling for recognition of adult literacy as a national issue and for government action – in effect calling for there to be a national policy. Then from the late 1990s there was the centralised Skills for Life initiative, a strong and well-resourced government policy. However, the traditions of student voice and of community involvement were almost eclipsed by Skills for Life. Now there is less central policy and less support for the field in relation to working with adults.

At the same time, in relation to schooling there is much more policy, in the sense of centralised instructions on what to do, associated with the teaching of reading and writing, with specific instructions about methods to be used. This 'advice' is not just addressed to teachers in classrooms, but is also aimed at parents at home, in ways which would have been unimaginable even twenty years ago.

Alongside developments in policy, throughout this period there have been significant developments in theories of what literacy is, that is perceptions and corresponding changes in classroom practice. This is an important aspect of the discussion in this book and the changes most elaborated here are social theories of literacy; how literacy can be seen as a set of social practices; and how the ways in which people make sense of literacy drives what they do.

In an everyday sense, the word *literacy* has meant being able to read and write, sometimes emphasising the reading aspect and sometimes emphasising the writing, but it is also intensely situated: a person has to be reading and writing something, and doing it somewhere and for some purpose. The chapters of the book are good in situating literacy, taking the discussion in quite different directions. In Chapter 4 what is going on in England is set in a context of international testing which has become more widespread and more influential. The traditional field of adult literacy is juxtaposed with academic literacy on the one hand in Chapter 5, and on the other with workplace literacy in Chapter 6. These are examples of the specific literacies argued for in Chapter 2 in relation to developing a curriculum. Many chapters of the book also take into account developments over time in the available technologies for reading and writing including changing notions of information literacy in Chapter 7. Drawing attention to these different sites makes it clear that it is essential to talk in the plural and refer to there being different *literacies*. Although focussing mainly on adults, the book also has a comparison with young people's contemporary literacies, as in Chapter 8.

In these rich discussions across different areas of literacy research and in keeping with the spirit of the book, it is probably worth reiterating the question *What is literacy?* First, there are the definitions which keep close to the acts of reading and writing. But even these are not straightforward since notions of what is meant by reading or writing are fluid and changing, especially when considered in relation to new technologies and online activities. Where does an act of reading start online and does it include searching, linking and navigating the multimodal layout of a web page? Similarly, does writing include the design and creation of online texts, and can the two terms be kept separate anyway? Far richer notions of reading and writing are used, for example by Sheridan and Rowsell (2010) and many others. Related to this, the changing relation of reading and writing and the growing significance of writing is argued persuasively by Deborah Brandt (2009).

The term literacy can keep close to reading and writing and can address how these activities are situated in specific areas, so that Chapter 5 addresses 'academic literacy' as the reading and writing needed for academic work, and Chapter 6 draws attention to 'workplace literacy' as the reading and writing in a specific workplace. Beyond these areas, the term literacy has come to be used in more metaphorical ways, such as in referring to someone as 'politically literate', 'emotionally literate', 'computer literate' and so on. These uses have the sense of knowing about, being competent in and knowledgeable in an area. This is a much broader use than the narrower idea of the dynamics of reading and writing. People find these metaphors useful and the idea of being literate, or illiterate, in an area has spread. I find it useful, but it may be worth examining the extent to which one is using the term metaphorically. It is significant whether or not someone uses the term *literacy* and, including the shift to the plural *literacies*. We could return to academic literacy and workplace literacy, for instance, and find elements of this broader metaphorical use.

Such discussions raise questions for the different areas covered in the book. In the uses of the term *literacy*, for example when thinking about 'information literacy', it may be worth thinking about the extent to which this is a metaphor and how much it has moved from being about reading and writing. Related to this what happens if we take the plural word 'literacies' as used by Lynn Coleman and Mary R. Lea in Chapter 5 when discussing academic literacies, and see what happens if we start talking in terms of 'information literacies' in the plural rather than the singular information literacy. To give another example of the choice of terms, when supporting students in college in their reading and writing, many different words for the field are used, each resonating with different theories. Is it 'study skills', 'academic writing', 'writing for academic purposes', or 'academic literacies'? Each suggests different ways of thinking about the field and different ways of supporting students.

To me the value of this book is the different approaches it puts next to each other. It enriches the field of adult literacy education by putting discussions of its future directions in the context of what is going on in related fields. The framing of the three Ps is the starting point and it provides part of a language of description based on practice, policy and perceptions. So what happens if we put a discussion of adult literacy next to discussions in these other areas, such as academic writing or information literacy? Ways of talking about literacy have developed in different ways in these fields and I hope that one of the outcomes of this book is that such a dialogue can take place. The examples chosen in the different chapters are interesting in their own right. Several broaden what we mean by reading and writing, and the multimodal example of academic literacy where the pedagogy involves actual film production. What interests me particularly is how most chapters of the book naturally work through multimodal examples, often based on new technologies. It may be useful for adult literacy education to think more in terms of multimodal texts as a space for developing literacy. Understanding adult literacy can also draw upon discussions going on in the field of academic literacies about the recontextualisation of texts and practices which goes on between the everyday and the educational, and also how practices need to go in the other direction, from the educational to the everyday.

To get these dialogues going, I would like to point to four other words beginning with 'p' which are used in the book: these are *pedagogy*, *participation*, *power* and *purposes*. These can help provide a broader common language of description. Like the original three Ps, *policy*, *perceptions* and *practice*, these additional four Ps are everyday words which have been sharpened up and defined more closely by being taken up in discussions of literacy.

As pointed out in the first two chapters, the perceptions and theories around literacy lead to different decisions about the teaching and other support needed, that is, different pedagogies. This is explored closely by Gordon Ade-Ojo in Chapter 2 and discussion of pedagogy recurs in later chapters. Just take one phrase, used by Guy Merchant in Chapter 8 in discussions of young children's development, that of 'parental pedagogies'. This phrase stands out as it suddenly removes the idea of pedagogies from its comfort zone of being closely related to education. It makes the point that families and others are involved in the support of literacy, in both informal and more formal ways. Maybe this idea from child literacy is actually of great value when thinking about issues of adult literacy education: adults have a range of support beyond the classroom and the idea of pedagogy can take on new meanings.

Moving on to the second term, *participation*, there is discussion of community involvement, particularly by John Crawford in Chapter 7 and specifically the importance of communities of practice by Mark Hepworth in Chapter 6, both in relation to information literacy. A crucial aspect of this approach is to emphasise the ways in which people participate in communities of practices. They can participate in different ways and change the ways in which they participate. For example, if new to a community it is often okay to stay on the edge and to silently observe what is going on, and often there are ways of trying out ways of acting and experimenting – learning involves changing ways of participating. Groups may differ in the ways they allow such spaces and it is important to accept that not all groupings of people are communities of practice. Especially online, there are affinity groups which people move in and out of more easily and do not have the seeming stability of community groups. People participate in different ways and these groups can be important for learning (see Barton & Lee 2013).

Third, most literacy events are assertions of power and the aim of empowerment underlies many approaches to adult literacy education. *Power* is central in many of the chapters of this book, with examples from workplaces and from academic life. The exercise of power is shown most graphically with international testing, in Chapter 4 by Mary Hamilton. In this broader picture we see the exercise of power where, through national government policies, international tests become the framing for what is taught and how it is taught. Looking more closely at the examples used by Vicky Duckworth in Chapter 3, pedagogy, participation and power can be seen working together. These examples show people learning by participating and by changing how they participate in the classes. This is done through their changing use of reading and writing. We see power exercised in the close detail of specific literacy events and how individual students become empowered by being involved in community publishing.

Finally, *purposes* are important and chapters have stressed the importance of people's purposes, noting how teachers' purposes of educational outcomes may differ from, for example, librarians' purposes which might be more concerned with social inclusion. Different participants may have different purposes. In taking account of students' purposes there is a reassertion of students' voices and the power of writing narratives. Ultimately, as in the examples of Chapter 3, it is people's everyday purposes which are central, and this is an essential component of a social practice pedagogy in adult literacy education.

## References

Barton, D. & C. Lee (2013) *Language online: Investigating digital texts and practices.* London: Routledge.

Brandt, D. (2009) *Literacy and learning: Reflections on writing, reading, and society.* San Fransisco: Jossey-Bass.

Sheridan, M. P. & J. Rowsell (2010) *Design literacies: Learning and innovation in the digital age.* London: Routledge.

# Index